LITERACY, POWER AND
SOCIAL JUSTICE

LITERACY, POWER AND SOCIAL JUSTICE

Adrian Blackledge

Trentham Books

First published in 2000 by Trentham Books Limited

Trentham Books Limited
Westview House
734 London Road
Oakhill
Stoke on Trent
Staffordshire
England ST4 5NP

British Cataloguing in Publication Data
A catalogue record for this book is available from the
British Library
ISBN 1 85856 157 4 (hb ISBN 1 85856 158 2)

Designed and typeset by Trentham Print Design Ltd., Chester and printed in Great Britain by Bell & Bain Ltd., Glasgow.

Contents

Chapter 1
THE SOCIAL PROCESS OF LITERACY • 1

Chapter 2
LITERACY AT HOME AND SCHOOL • 23

Chapter 3
PARENTAL INVOLVEMENT IN CHILDREN'S READING IN MULTILINGUAL CONTEXTS • 41

Chapter 4
BANGLADESHI CHILDREN'S READING AT HOME AND SCHOOL • 61

Chapter 5
INVOLVING MINORITY-LANGUAGE PARENTS AT SCHOOL • 89

Chapter 6
MULTILINGUAL LITERACIES AT HOME AND SCHOOL • 109

Chapter 7
INVOLVING MINORITY-LANGUAGE PARENTS IN POLICY AND PRACTICE • 127

References • 147

Index • 157

Acknowledgements

I would like to thank the children of Valley Community Primary School, and their families and teachers, for allowing me to intrude on their homes and classrooms. I am grateful to Deirdre Martin, Aneta Pavlenko, Ingrid Piller and Marya Teutsch-Dwyer for their advice and encouragement in the development of this project. Any errors are, of course, my own.

I owe most to Bernie Murray, and our children Sam, Jessie and Joel, for their considerable and continuing patience and support.

1

THE SOCIAL PROCESS OF LITERACY

One of the major tasks for schools in the twenty-first century is to teach all students to be literate. In this simple statement is a world of complexity. What does it mean to be literate? How do we define literacy? Is literacy the same for everyone, or can there be many co-existent literacies? Is literacy learned only in schools, or is literacy also learned in students' homes and communities? If this is so, how should schools respond? What is the importance of literacy in terms of cultural and personal identity? What role does literacy play in societies where there are unequal relations of power between different groups? How does literacy interact with language use for minority language speakers in majority language contexts? If schools are important sites of social and cultural reproduction (Heller, 1999) what is the role of literacy in the process of schooling?

These are the questions which shape this book. In a multicultural and multilingual society there are many and diverse literacies which have different meanings for different groups and individuals. When schools respond positively to the literacies of their communities, much can be done to reverse the inequalities which are so often evident in relations between dominant and minority groups. By involving parents and other family and community members in the teaching and learning of literacy, and by building on the existing literacies of family and community, schools can act as catalysts in a process of empowerment for children, their families and their teachers. That is, collaborative literacy teaching and learning can be a positive force in the redefinition of relations of power, and the enhancement of social justice.

In the first part of this book I set out a model of literacy teaching and learning which is based on the existing literacies of linguistic minority children and their families. In the second, I report a recent study of the literacy support practices of Bangladeshi parents in an urban setting in Britain as they tried to help their children to become proficient in school and community literacies. The voices of the Bangladeshi parents, and their children's teachers, make clear the attitudes, expectations and frustrations involved in the literacy learning process when the majority-culture educators attempted to involve minority-culture parents in their children's education. In addition to the interview responses of the teachers and parents, the home and school literacy learning process can be traced in audio-cassette recordings of the Bangladeshi children reading with support at home and at school.

Literacy or literacies?

Recent research has found that literacy and literacies are many and varied in their forms and uses. In this first chapter I present literacy and literacies as complex cultural practices rather than a discrete set of individual skills. I propose that literacy is a socially constructed phenomenon which has different meanings for different societies, and for different cultural groups within societies. I consider literacy in terms of culturally meaningful literacy interactions (for example, teachers or family members listening to children read) which occur within 'zones of proximal development' (Vygotsky, 1978), and in the context of relations of power between majority and minority groups in society. A central aspect of these relations of power refers to the interface between cultural identity and literacy learning.

Literacy as cultural practices

A crucial debate among literacy researchers concerns whether to view literacy as a set of *individual skills*, or as *cultural practices*. In the former, literacy is thought of as something universal, which people carry around in their heads from setting to setting, task to task. This model assumes that literacy processes are only marginally affected by the social contexts in which they occur. In the latter model literacy is conceived as a set of social or cultural practices, and its participants as a *community of practice* (Reder, 1994). The *individual skills* model sees literacy as a set of de-contextualised information processing skills, which the individual learns and then contextualises by applying them to a progressively wider range of activities. The *cultural practices* model is useful for addressing the ways in which literacy behaviours are closely fitted to and vary with the contexts in which they occur. The *cultural practices* model sees literacy skills and knowledge developing directly within specific contexts of practice that vary across languages and cultures. These views of literacy are not contradictory – they complement each other. The practices of literacy, what they are and what they mean for a given society, depend on the context. The skills and concepts that accompany literacy learning do not stem in some automatic way from the inherent qualities of print, but are aspects of the specific uses of and approaches to literacy that are implicit within the social, political and intellectual forces that constitute that society (Langer, 1987). Thus, literacy may not have the same meaning in minority-culture households and dominant-culture households in Britain, or in minority-culture households and dominant-culture schools.

There is an apparent tension between a model which views literacy as a psychological process, and one which views literacy as a social process. However, literacy cannot be considered to be *either* psychological *or* social, but as an integration of processes operating on both of these levels (Scribner, 1987). External social factors affect the internalisation of cognitive gains through literacy. The development of the mental operations involved in reading and writing cannot be fully understood without also understanding the contexts in which literacy is experienced. Literacy is not a universal that is achieved spontaneously. Rather, it is a cultural achievement (Teale and Sulzby, 1987). The *cultural practices* model assumes that the development of an individual's literacy is shaped by the structure and organisation of the social situations in which literacy is encountered and practised. Literacy development is driven by qualities of individuals' engagement in particular literacy practices (Reder, 1994). A critical issue in this model, whether in or out of school, concerns what it is about literacy interactions that produces (or fails to produce) gains in literacy. If collaborative activities are critical contexts for literacy development, then the social structure of those situations is likely to have a substantial influence on the development process.

Literacies at home

Until recently there has often been an assumption among educators and policy-makers that the homes of poor, minority-culture families are less effective language and literacy learning environments than the homes of middle-class, majority-culture families. Minority groups are massively over-represented among the 'functionally illiterate' in Western developed countries (Cummins, 1994a). But public discourse often absolves schools and society from responsibility for minority-group underachievement, and attributes school failure to the students' own deficiencies (lack of academic effort), or deficiencies of their families (parental inadequacy).

However, careful observational research indicates that these assumptions are unfounded. Anderson and Stokes (1984), Delgado-Gaitan (1990) and others have studied literacy practices in the homes of families from a range of ethnic and linguistic backgrounds. Anderson and Stokes found a wide range of language learning activities in the homes of African-American, Mexican-American and Anglo-American families, most of which were unrelated to school work. In her study of Mexican-American families, Delgado-Gaitan found that much literacy learning in the home takes place on a moment-to-moment basis, including both those processes that are deliberate, systematic and sustained, and those fleeting actions that take place at the margins of awareness. Despite the fact that the parents in Delgado-Gaitan's study had little prior schooling and did not perceive themselves as readers, they regularly used texts in English and Spanish (e.g. newspapers, letters from relatives) as an integral part of daily life. Several studies (e.g. Auerbach, 1989; Ada, 1988) have refuted the notion that poor, minority-culture families fail to value or support their children's literacy development. In fact quite the opposite seems to be the case for many immigrant groups: those families most marginalised frequently see literacy and schooling as the key to mobility, to changing their status and preventing their children from suffering as they did.

Literacy does not necessarily have the same meaning or function in all societies, or in all communities within a society. Literacy is not only being able to read and write but being able to utilise these skills in a socially appropriate context (Delgado-Gaitan, 1990). That is, in understanding literacies in communities and societies, we should ask what are the *purposes* of literacy. For example, the complex English literacy practices required of Welsh-speaking dairy farmers in Wales as they struggle to come to terms with European legislation are significantly different from those of their fathers and grandfathers who worked the same land (Jones, in press). Martin-Jones and Bhatt (1998) give a further example of a 20-year-old Kenyan immigrant to Britain who taught herself to read and write Gujarati so she could write to relatives back home. Many other examples suggest that literacy development is different for different groups in a society, and for different families and individuals within those groups. Development of an individual's literacy is shaped by the structure and organisation of the social situations in which literacy is practised (Reder, 1994).

Literacy activities cannot be divorced from larger political, economic and cultural forces in a given society. Neither their structures nor their function can be understood outside of their societal context (Scribner, 1987). In multilingual settings roles and social meanings should be understood with respect to language and literacy choices. For example, in some communities in USA, becoming literate in native Spanish language carries negative meanings (in contrast to the positive meanings attached to becoming literate in English), even though spoken use of Spanish is preferred in most situations. Among Hmong refugees in USA, on the other hand, there are positive social meanings associated with developing literacy initially in the native language, just as there are positive reasons for different Asian groups in Britain to become literate in their community languages (Saxena, 1991; Gregory, 1996a). A historical perspective is provided by de Castell, Luke and Egan (1986), who argue that in order to understand literacy, the personal, social and political context in which literacy occurs must be explicitly addressed. Literacy does not simply consist of a universally defined set of skills constant across time and place. In seeking to maximise literacy learning opportunities for all students, it is important that schools and policy-makers identify the social functions, meanings and values attached to literacy in particular communities.

Literacies at school

The functions, meanings and values which are attached to literacy by schools may be different from those held by the communities they serve.

This is less likely for middle-class, majority-culture children attending majority schools, where there will most probably be continuity in the perceptions and uses of literacy in the school and the home. For minority-culture families the picture is often more complex. Since authority is vested in those belonging to the mainstream culture, the literacy practices of the mainstream become the norm and have higher status in school contexts. One explanation for the relative success in school of middle-class, majority-language children is that their home environments provide them with the kind of literacy skills and practices needed to do well in school. The fact that their parents use and transmit literacy in the specific ways that schools expect gives these children an advantage (Heath, 1983; Auerbach, 1989). This is not to imply that the language environments provided by working-class and/or minority-culture homes is deficient. It suggests, rather, that the culture of schools may be favourable to certain groups at the expense of others.

In educating children towards literacy, schools vary in the extent to which they incorporate and take account of the cultural views and values of the ethnic groups to which the children belong. To the extent that schools tend to reflect the dominant culture, children from the majority group are more likely than minority-culture students to find consistency and continuity between home and school constructs of literacy (Ferdman, 1990). When these constructs are similar, there is little need for anyone to attend to the process of cultural transmission. However, for minority-culture children it is most likely that to become successful in school literacy they will have to learn and play by the rules of a culture which is skewed in favour of the white middle-class (Knight, 1994). The increased standardisation and uniformity of a skills-based approach to literacy instruction at the expense of meaningful interpretation of text fails to acknowledge the differences between school and home literacy values and practices, thus making it more difficult for those who do not share the dominant culture to become literate (de Castell and Luke, 1987).

Literacy in the school and the home can be understood at two levels: (i) literacy interactions can be analysed in terms of their cultural meanings for the individuals involved (Heath, 1983; Cummins, 1994a), and (ii) at a broader level, literacy in the home and school can be interpreted in terms of relations of power in the society in which they occur. We now consider the role of culture, and then relations of power in literacy learning.

The role of culture in literacy interactions

Minority-culture families living in poor socioeconomic conditions often face sustained isolation from the school culture, which can lead to mis-communication between parents and school (Delgado-Gaitan, 1991). Schools facilitate the exclusion of students and parents by (consciously or unconsciously) establishing activities that require specific majority cul-turally based knowledge and behaviours. Frequently, the need for this knowledge is not made explicit. The absence of such knowledge pre-cludes acceptable participation in formal school activities, resulting in isolation for many parents, especially those minority-culture parents who have not been schooled in the host country. Where sociocultural con-gruence exists between home and school settings, children have a greater chance of succeeding in school. Parents who are knowledgeable about the school's expectations and how the school operates may be better advocates for their children than those who are not. Analysis of formal and informal home and school literacy activities can provide a window on the extent to which cultural congruence exists between the dominant school and the minority-culture home.

Heath's (1983) ethnographic study of three rural communities in the Pied-mont Carolinas, USA found a broad range of uses of literacy in the homes of white working-class, black working-class, and mainly white middle-class families. The relationship between home and school practices was significant. The mainstream 'Townspeople' group prepared their children for school through a range of literacy activities which resembled those found in the schools, including labelling, describing events, answering questions, reading books and playing with educational toys. The 'Townspeople' parents assumed that what happens at school and at home is linked, and they made possible a variety of activities and resources to support these links. Parents would ask their children questions about school, and find ways to make links between home and school. Dis-continuities between out-of-school activities and in-school lessons occurred for individuals, but not for the group as a whole. Most of the children from Townspeople homes did well in school. The black working-class Trackton parents engaged their pre-school children in a broad range of literacy activities, including storytelling, sharing rhymes, songs and church-related literacy. However, arrival in school would bring a sudden flood of discontinuities in the way people talk, the values they hold, and the consistency with which rewards go to some children and not others. Trackton children fell quickly into a pattern of school failure. The white working-class Roadville parents prepared their children for school through coaching them in book-reading, and colouring-book sessions at the kitchen-table. Roadville children went to school imbued with testimony about the value of reading, but with few models of reading and writing behaviour. After initial success, Roadville children would fall behind the mainstream Townspeople children. Heath concluded that it was not the quantity of talk in the home that was significant, but the extent to which there was continuity or discontinuity between school and home in the literacy and language activities carried out in those settings.

Cultural compatibility in literacy learning

Researchers investigating cultural compatibility between learning environments at home and at school have studied the ways in which the teaching and learning of minority-culture children occurs, and have introduced changes in schools to make the curriculum more compatible with those strengths (Au, 1980). When children possess the cultural repertoires upon which school depends, all goes well. When cultures provide some other set of social and psychological routines, schools and pupils can become mutually frustrated. Tharp (1989) argues that in order to ensure continuity between school and home, teaching should occur in a context and process that is compatible with the natal culture of the students. That is, the responsibility to change lies with the school rather than the home. A major source of the cultural compatibility model was the development of the Kamehameha Early Education Programme (KEEP), a language-arts programme initially for children of Hawaiian ancestry (Au, 1980) in USA, which was later transferred to a very different Navajo setting. In developing a programme which tailored classrooms to children, four features of schools were identified which may be changed: social organisation, sociolinguistics, cognition and motivation.

Cultural differences in *motivation* are central variables in school achievement. In Hawaiian society children are generally much more peer-oriented than adult-oriented. This leads to chaos in some classrooms when they begin school, as children are not used to interaction with adults.

Hawaiian children understand an explicit system of rewards and punishments. Navajo children, on the other hand, are managed in their communities by contingencies of only the most general kind, through reiteration of cultural values rather than by expressions of displeasure which mention specific children. In Navajo society children live in close association with adults. So when they arrive in school they expect to interact with adults. In both Navajo and Hawaiian KEEP classrooms teachers maintain orderly, motivated learning environments; but they do so by very different patterns in their own behaviour and in their relationships with children.

A second variable is the *social organisation* of the classroom. Small-group orientation is strong among Hawaiian children and adults and is deeply rooted in the natal culture, where collaboration, cooperation and assisted performance are common in everyday experience. Hawaiian children tend to have problems adjusting to classrooms that emphasise large group activity settings, in which they are expected to perform independently and orient to a single adult. In Navajo culture, however, children are expected to perform independently at an early age. Also, from the age of about eight boys and girls are expected not to play together. In Hawaiian KEEP classrooms the optimum group was made up of four to five boys and girls. In Navajo KEEP classrooms the most effective and independent groups were composed of two to three children of the same sex. These models of social organisation proved to be successful for learning in their respective settings.

The *sociolinguistic* features studied in the cultural compatibility movement are primarily the courtesies and conventions of conversation. Navajo children, for example, are used to conversation which is characterised by turn-taking, listening, and measured pauses before response is made. For Hawaiian children on the other hand, formal turn-taking is not expected, as they engage in conversational patterns which produce overlapping speech. Teachers who are not aware of these patterns may inadvertently interrupt Navajo children, or silence Hawaiian children by insisting on formal turn-taking. In ordinary classrooms Hawaiian children respond in a minimal way when teachers address them. The rich verbal routines of their home culture almost never appear in such classrooms, nor do long, connected narratives. The Hawaiian KEEP programme developed text-based discussion groups which allowed children to use the broad range of their language repertoire. In ordinary schools Navajo children are quiet, abrupt, and not verbally engaged by teachers' question and answer sessions. In their home culture the children are used to listening quietly to frequent, lengthy storytelling. The Navajo KEEP programme encourages children to talk and listen at length, as they articulate their ideas. Teachers of Navajo children who frequently interrupt narrative events with questions produce a sharp cultural incongruity.

Tharp also reports evidence that specific *cognitive* abilities are characteristic of Native American groups, for example the importance of visual rather than verbal processes in perception and representation, and holistic rather than analytic processes in thinking and learning. This is the opposite of regular education, which is almost exclusively analytic and overwhelmingly verbal. In KEEP's Experience-Text-Relationship method of teaching reading, the teacher stimulates the students to speak or think of their relevant personal experiences before introducing text material, and after a period of concentrating on the text, the relationship between experience and text is explored. Contextualising formal material in personal, community-based experiences is not merely cosmetic but provides the cognitive links that allow students to grasp literacy. In the struggle for identity that minority-culture children must undertake, contextualisation allows them to accommodate to school while remaining anchored in the natal culture. Children bring to school a range of different experiences and expectations of literacy interactions, all firmly rooted in the culture of the home, and which may or may not be consistent with the experiences and expectations of literacy they encounter in schools. Children who find continuity between school and home literacy practices are more likely to become literate in the terms prescribed by the school. The literacy interactions which occur in the learning process are crucial in determining whether or not literacy learning is culturally meaningful for the child.

Culturally meaningful interactions in literacy learning

In literacy learning, as in other contexts, children learn knowledge and skills through interactions with more able adults and peers. Through their interaction with children, adults (and more able peers or older children) mediate the construction of meaning by helping to create with children the interpersonal conditions within which they can learn. These learning interactions are successful to the extent that they are meaningful to the child; they can be viewed within the framework of Vygotsky's (1978) *zone of proximal development* (ZPD). Vygotsky identified the ZPD as the distance between children's developmental level as determined by individual problem solving without adult guidance, and the level of potential development as determined by children's problem solving under the influence of, or in collaboration with, more capable adults or peers. Put simply, the ZPD is the interactional or interpersonal space where minds meet and new understandings can arise through collaborative inter-action and inquiry (Cummins, 1996). Newman, Griffin and Cole (1989) call this interactional space the *construction zone*. Vygotsky viewed language as crucial for the development of thinking skills, and language control as a measure of mental development. His emphasis on the learner's role in determining his/her area of greatest possible cognitive development through culturally meaningful interaction is related to the role that culture plays in communication during learning activities.

The concept of ZPD assumes that higher, distinctively human psycho-logical functions have sociocultural origins (Newman, Griffin and Cole, 1989). The activities that constitute a construction zone *are* the social origins referred to; when cognitive change occurs not only what is carried out in the interaction but *how* the participants carry it out provides the social context for learning. Consequently, the cultural and social context of learning is essential to the acquisition and organisation of concepts (Trueba, 1989).The culturally mediated interaction among the people in the construction zone is internalised, becoming a new function of the learner. Another way to say it is that the interpsychological (learning in the social plane) becomes also intrapsychological (learning in the mental plane). Children learn higher level skills as they engage in socially meaningful literacy activities. They first learn the activity in a social setting in which cultural interpretations are embedded and communicated by other members of the society, and with experience they internalise the skills needed to complete the activity, and also the socially or culturally accepted way to evaluate the meaning and relative success of that activity.

Culture plays a crucial role in how a learner gains access to the signs and symbols in the environment and learns to imbue them with meaning. The signs of a culture, the symbols of that culture, and the meanings (how to read that culture) are all accomplished first in interaction with others, and later internalised for personal use (Langer, 1987). Literacy and cultural development are inextricably bound, and learning a new literacy therefore requires learners to become 'bicultural'. The ZPD can be observed in classrooms and apprenticeship settings, as well as in non-institutional settings such as mother-child interaction and children's play. It cannot be viewed as a place outside of the experiences and expectations children bring to school from home. Culturally meaningful interactions between participants in the construction zone can only be fully understood in the context of structures of power and interpretations of identity which prevail in society.

Literacy and cultural identity

Cultural identity may be understood at group and individual levels (Ferdman, 1990). A group's cultural identity involves a shared sense of the cultural features that help define and characterise the group, such as religious life. If features central to the group's cultural identity are viewed negatively by the larger society, the group may incorporate a negative component into its self-evaluation. Individual members of groups will vary both in the extent of their identification with the group and in the degree to which their behaviour is based on the group's cultural norms; some may be willing to adopt some of the cultural practices of the majority, while others refuse to do so. There will always be diversity within any cultural group. Cultural identity therefore includes the individual's internalised view of the cultural features characteristic of their group plus the value that the person attaches to those features. Minority group members may choose, or sometimes be forced, to adopt aspects of the majority culture in order to succeed in mainstream society.

Because literacy is a culturally defined construct, it should have close links to cultural identity (Ferdman, 1990). When literacy is transferred from a dominant culture to a minority-culture which has not historically been literate, majority culture values will be transmitted as part of the 'package' of literacy (Street, 1987). In order to acquire literacy in the majority language the learner will have to adopt some of the cultural behaviours and values of the majority and risk sacrificing cultural group identity. De Castell and Luke (1987) contend that this process is calculated by majority groups, so that in literacy campaigns reading and writing are secondary concerns, and the primary purpose of institutionally transmitted literacy is rather the creation of a shared sociocultural world view. That is, the aim of such programmes is to construct and disseminate a dominant national ideology rather than develop bicultural skills essential for minorities to succeed in majority settings.

If the acquisition of majority-culture literacy in a minority-culture context requires the adoption of some of the cultural behaviours and values of the majority group, people are faced with choices that may have implications for their identity as a member of the minority cultural group. Students must either adopt the perspective of the school (and therefore the majority society), at the risk of developing a negative component to their cultural identity, or else resist the pressure to adopt the majority values and behaviours and risk becoming alienated from the school. For majority-culture children, on the other hand, the school's perspective is likely to be consistent with their existing cultural identity.

Matute-Bianchi (1986) shows that for minority-culture group members, perceptions of themselves and their cultural identity in relation to other minority-culture group members are significant in determining their attitudes to school-related activities. Among five groups of Mexican-descent students in California, two ('Mexicans' and 'Mexican-Americans') considered school success to be not incompatible with their cultural identity. 'Mexicans' were typically born in Mexico, and retained pride in Mexican heritage. 'Mexican-Americans' were typically born in the US, identified themselves as Americans of Mexican descent, and saw themselves as more American oriented than the 'Mexicans'. As they learned the dominant culture of the school, these groups did not believe that they had to give up important parts of their identity. For other groups ('Chicanos' and 'Cholos') the picture was quite different. 'Chicanos' were characterised by loyalty to their group and their choice of specific cultural symbols, for example listening to non-mainstream music. Chicanos would describe academically successful Mexican-descent students as 'Wannabes', meaning that they 'want to be white'. Students in this group might want to do well in school but nonetheless behave in ways that promote failure: frequent absences, failure to do homework, disruptive behaviour. The 'Cholo' group was distinguished by stylistic symbols which identified them as gang members, and were looked down on by other Mexican-descent students. They were neither active participants in school activities nor usually regarded as successful students. To be a Chicano or Cholo meant not participating in school in ways that would promote academic success and achievement.

Matute-Bianchi describes the Chicano and Cholo groups as 'castelike': they would resist features of the school culture, especially the behavioural patterns required for school success. To adopt these cultural features, e.g. to participate in school activities and strive to do well in school, was viewed derisively within the group. Thus these students were forced to choose: do well in school or risk losing their cultural group identity. In Ogbu's (1987) terms, the Chicanos and Cholos had developed an identity in opposition to the cultural frame of reference demanded by the mainstream society. For them school learning was the learning of white people. To adopt these behaviours was to abandon their own cultural frame of reference.

Matute-Bianchi also interviewed Japanese-American students – who were clear that being identified as a Japanese-American meant that they were considered to be smart, hard-working, well-behaved and studious. Except for their physical appearance, they saw themselves, and were seen by others, as virtually indistinguishable from the successful, accomplished, well-dressed Anglo students in the school. So these students had no difficulty, dilemma or opposition to participating in the school community.

Community literacies

One of the ways in which new minority groups have sought to maintain their languages has been through the development of community language schools. Saxena (1994) reports that Panjabi parents in Britain who recognised the threat of loss of language and cultural values in their communities made a concerted effort to open temples where children could learn and appreciate their culture, religions and languages. Saxena (1991) found that Panjabis in Southall were motivated by religious or nationalistic ideology to have their children learn literacies of the home country. For example, learning to read the Gurmukhi script was symbolic of the Sikh nation, while learning to read Davanagari script represented a commitment to Hindu cultural identity. In Australia, by far the largest number of ethnic schools are Greek (Clyne, 1982). These tend to be held several afternoons a week after day school, although there are also Greek Sunday schools. The USA supports community language schools for a broad range of languages. Fishman (1989, 1991) found, however, that their constituency was less the non-English speaking immigrant child than the native-born child with a non-English speaking background. That is, the children were sent to the schools as a means to avoid language loss. But the language schools may be of value to minority communities as more than a means to maintain languages. Some children will receive instruction in a language other than the spoken language of the home. Gregory (1996b) reports that English/Sylheti bilingual Bangladeshi children in London go to community schools (which may in fact be held in neighbours' houses) to learn standard Bengali, and go to a local mosque to learn to read Arabic, the language of the Qur'an. The Linguistic Minorities Project (1985) found that a similar situation existed in British Pakistani communities: children went to community schools to learn to read and write Urdu, the standard language of Pakistan, although their home language may have been non-standard and regional, e.g Pushto or Mirpuri.

The children were sent to community schools not to avoid loss of the home language, as it was not the home language that was being taught but a standard form. In these cases it may be that language had a significance beyond the instrumental. Farah (1998) notes that the meaning of Qur'anic literacy for Muslims lies not entirely in interpretation of the text but is rather symbolically related to the Qur'an being the word of God, and 'sounding it out' is itself a blessed act. Taylor (1998) reports that many Chinese parents in Britain send their school-age children to supplementary schools on weekends in community centres, church halls or regular school buildings. Chinese teachers, most of them not trained to teach Chinese as a second language, work as unpaid volunteers. A smaller number of Japanese Saturday schools caters for the smaller Japanese community in Britain (Taylor, 1998).

Relations of power in literacy learning

Street (1984) proposed the term 'autonomous model' of literacy to describe theories which treat literacy as an independent variable, somehow divorced from the social and ideological contexts that give it meaning. This model assumes that the social consequences of literacy are given, and schools need only address the question of how literacy is to be taught. But other questions should be addressed before the apparently technical ones, questions derived from an alternative, 'ideological' model of literacy which focuses on the social and cultural practices of reading and writing. The 'ideological' model recognises the culturally embedded nature of literacy practices and is concerned with the socialisation process in the construction of meaning. The model goes even further, locating literacy not only in the context of culture but also within power structures in society.

Ogbu (1987) suggests that the real issue in the acquisition of literacy for minorities is not whether children possess a different language or dialect, a different communication style, a different participation structure or interaction style, or a different pattern of language socialisation and upbringing. The crucial variables are, firstly, whether or not the children come from a segment of society where people have traditionally experienced unequal opportunity to use their literacy skills in a socially and economically meaningful manner and, secondly, whether or not the relationship between the minorities and dominant-group members who control the education system has encouraged minorities to perceive and define acquisition of literacy as an instrument of deculturation without true assimilation. Ogbu points out that minority groups in any society differ from one another and so defy generalisations. He identifies three types of minority group: *autonomous minorities*, who are not socially, economically or politically subordinated; they tend not to have significant literacy problems because they have a cultural frame of reference which demonstrates and encourages school success; *immigrant minorities* – people who moved voluntarily to the host country because they believed it to be a place of greater opportunity and who may experience some school-related problems but not sustained failure; and *castelike* or *subordinate* minorities – people who originally moved to the host country involuntarily, through slavery, conquest or colonisation. It is this last group, says Ogbu, which has greatest problems acquiring literacy. Castelike minorities define their cultural identity in opposition to the cultural values of the mainstream, so cannot succeed in schooling.

However, Ogbu's analysis is perhaps simplistic in its distinctions. African-Caribbean people in Britain, for example, do not fit easily into this schema: are they ex-slaves or voluntary migrants? In fact there are almost certain to be differences within as well as between groups. Moreover, while there is merit in understanding the historical context of immigrant minorities, Zentella (1997) suggests that Ogbu's categories do not allow for within-group distinctions: 'involuntary castes and voluntary migrants are painted with too broad a brush stroke' (p.272). Also, Ogbu's model may create opportunities for stereotyping, as it seems to deny that some individuals succeed in even the most 'castified' group (Trueba, 1993b). In addition, Ogbu seems to locate literacy learning *only* in the school, giving the impression that there is only one social meaning for literacy in a cultural group (Reder, 1994).

But reservations about the application of this model should not deny its contribution to an expanded understanding of the role of macro-social factors that may prevent full and successful participation of some minorities in social institutions, including schools (Trueba, 1993b). Cummins (1994a) agrees that contributory factors to some minority group underachievement derive from the sociohistorical relations between dominant and minority groups. These macro-interactions appear to result in the internalisation by the minority groups of a sense of ambivalence about their cultural identity and a sense of powerlessness in relation to the dominant group.

Cultural and critical literacies

Approaches to literacy instruction that focus only on technical skills of reading and writing are unlikely to succeed (Cummins, 1994b). To be effective, school literacy instruction should address the root causes of illiteracy, including unjust relations of power in society. Intervention should encourage students to challenge dominant group constructions of the cultural identity of the minority group. Cummins distinguishes between *functional, cultural* and *critical* literacy instruction. Teaching functional literacy implies a level of reading and writing that enables people to function adequately in society and, as such, is defined relative to changing societal demands. Functional literacy implies a set of cognitive skills that enables individuals to function in social and employment situations in their society. *Cultural literacy* emphasises the need for shared experiences within an interpretive community in order to adequately comprehend texts. Whereas functional literacy focuses on skills, cultural literacy instruction emphasises the content or knowledge required for interpreting text in particular cultural contexts. These distinctions are not absolute: 'functioning' in social and employment situations involves drawing on specific cultural practices. The key point here is that in terms of pedagogy, a cultural literacy approach seeks to build on cultural practices and expand the cultural knowledge of the student. *Critical literacy* goes further, focusing on the potential of written language to be a tool for people to analyse the division of power and resources in their society and transform discriminatory structures. Practical examples of the 'critical literacy' approach with reference to the multilingual, multicultural classroom are set out in Chapter Six.

Literacy interactions either reinforce or challenge structures of power in school and society – teachers' talk to children about text can either reinforce existing relations of power in society or it can promote collaborative relations of power. In these interactions minority group students may be given a voice with which to respond to the world of the text and the world beyond the text, or they may be rendered voiceless in much the way that their communities have been disempowered through their interactions with societal institutions. Children from communities that have historically been subordinated may succeed educationally to the extent that the literacy interactions in school reverse the relations of power that prevail in the society at large (Cummins, 1994a). In accepting the notions of functional, cultural and critical literacies we must ask who determines what constitutes adequate functional literacy. In culturally diverse societies these decisions are more likely to be made by the dominant or majority culture.

Literacy and 'illiteracy'

Only those who have power can decide what constitutes 'literacy' (Freire and Macedo, 1987). Once the intellectual parameters are set, those who want to be considered literate must meet the requirements dictated by the dominant class. The literate activity of those without power is often defined as non-literate, yet some of those defined as 'illiterate' might be refusing to be literate as an act of resistance. Members of oppressed groups may consciously or unconsciously refuse to learn the specific cultural codes and competences authorised by the dominant culture's view of literacy (Giroux, 1987). 'Illiteracy' is therefore as much a social construction as 'literacy'. Since cultures differ in what they consider to be their 'texts' and the values they attach to them, they will also differ in what they regard as literate behaviour. The same person may be regarded as 'illiterate' by one cultural group yet quite literate by another. When a number of cultures co-exist within the same society a range of versions of what constitutes being literate is likely (Ferdman, 1990). The notion of 'illiteracy' has to be seen not as an objective description of social fact but as an ideological, historically located interpretation which is a product of specific interests and which constructs a group of people (Prinsloo and Breier, 1996).

Street and Street (1991) argue that 'school literacy' tends to define what counts as literacy, and that this constructs the lack of school literacy in deficit terms: those who are not literate in the terms determined by the school are seen as illiterate and so lacking essential skills. Adults who lack reading and writing skills are often judged to be intellectually, culturally and even morally inferior to others. Illiterate adults should be seen as members of oral sub-cultures with their own set of values and beliefs, rather than as failing members of the dominant society. Illiterate adults often see themselves as interdependent, rather than dependent, sharing their skills and knowledge with members of their social networks (Lytle and Landau, 1987).

Lankshear (1987) proposes that the social production of illiteracy is an important political process. He notes that in discussing people who are illiterate in Western societies the literature often talks about incompetence (of the individual, family, group, teacher or school) but not about injustice. The disadvantage of those who are not literate in the majority language is not seen as a consequence of the very structures by which others are advantaged, and enabled to maintain and extend their advantage. The small-scale school projects introduced to teach 'illiterate' individuals and groups to read often ignore the structures in society which maintain patterns of injustice. Lankshear argues that those who are 'illiterate' are usually situated at the wrong end of the continuum of structural power with respect to their economic, political and cultural interests. They may find it difficult to get employment, and if they do find work, it is likely to be poorly paid and low-status. Structured illiteracy seems to explain and legitimate (to the dominant and subordinate alike) iniquitous structures of power in society. The 'illiterate' are seen as economically disadvantaged because they lack literacy skills instead of the other way round.

In a study of the perceived illiteracy and actual literacy practices of South African taxi drivers (Breier, Matsepela and Sait, 1996), the drivers managed the paperwork required of their job without full and formal knowledge of the kind of literacy demanded by schools. They were widely referred to in official assessments as 'illiterate' and most had had little or no formal schooling. Yet in the course of their work the drivers were constantly dealing with situations which seemed to require reading and writing. They might have been considered illiterate within the auto-nomous model of literacy, but from a culturally sensitive perspective they clearly used literacy practices for specific purposes, in particular contexts (Street, 1996). Kell (1996) reports the case of an ANC activist who operated successfully in a literate environment for many years without be-coming literate as defined by the dominant culture. Once a literacy pro-gramme was put in place, she was designated 'illiterate' and internalised this view, so she perceived herself as illiterate. Although she was con-stantly involved in informal literacy practices and was undoubtedly literate in terms of her mastery of hegemonic discourses during the strug-gle against apartheid, in the terms of conventional schooled literacy she was regarded as a failure.

Gibson (1996) found that farm workers who might at first be labelled 'illiterate' were able to interpret and use complex instructional documents in order to build and maintain irrigation systems. Literacy practices among the 'Coloured' Afrikaans-speaking workers on three farms in the Western Cape were embedded in relations of power between worker and farmer and between men and women. Knowledge of farming was a male domain, accessible only to men. Knowledge of books was a female domain but despite the women's greater level of literacy, they were consigned to more menial jobs than the men. Some male farm workers were not literate in the conventional sense, yet their command of certain knowledge gave them access to power, whereas the higher level of 'schooled' literacy among the women did not. Being literate was not an important criterion for access to employment or power among this group. Being male was much more significant. These South African studies demonstrate that literacy and literacies have different meanings and functions for different groups, and that there is no single definition of what it means to be literate. However, for many groups, their literacies are marginalised and undervalued by those who have the power to decide which literacies have status in society.

Martin-Jones (1996) notes that women have remained largely invisible in research on bilingualism and literacy among minority language groups in Britain. She describes the language and literacy histories and practices of two Gujarati-speaking women who migrated to Leicester from Malawi and India, where both constructed new identities. In the process, the literacies learned in the country of origin became crucial symbolic resources. The Muslim woman who, through determination and commitment, gained an education in English in Malawi was able to use her English literacy to gain employment in England and to support the Gujarati community in Leicester and found a Gujarati women's group. The Hindu woman, who came to Leicester after she was married, had had the benefit of an education in Gujarati in India and had also learned English and been exposed to literacy in Hindi and Sanskrit. After moving to England, she ensured that her children learned both English and Gujarati. She qualified as a teacher and taught in a primary school, where she used her multiliteracies as a learning resource. She also took on the post of headteacher in a Gujarati Saturday school. The Martin-Jones (1996) study demonstrates that Asian women who migrate to Britain often have a range of language and literacy resources, many of which go unnoticed by institutions in British society. Minority-language women often draw on language and literacy resources to redefine their identities and to reshape cultural practices.

In Freire and Macedo's terms (1987) the person who *refuses* to become literate (as determined by the dominant group) as an act of resistance may be able to read the world (politically and culturally) very clearly, despite refusing to read the word (acquire technical skills). The 'illiteracy' of certain minority groups can perhaps be best understood not as skills deficiencies but as a refusal to internalise the values and attitudes of the literacy practices favoured by the dominant cultural group within society (Devine, 1994). Greater literacy does not necessarily correlate with increased equality and democracy, nor with better conditions for the working class (Street, 1984). Yet for these same migrants, as we have seen, an attempt to acquire literacy in the majority language may require them to put at risk their cultural identity.

Summary

This chapter has outlined a theoretical framework which views literacy as a social process in relation to both interactions with texts and structures of power in society. Literacy is more than a decontextualised set of skills. It is a socially constructed phenomenon which has different meanings for different groups in societies, and for individuals within those groups. Groups who have traditionally been regarded as lacking in literacy skills often provide rich language environments for their children but this wealth of resources may be at odds with the expectations of the school. School-based literacy interactions may create cultural continuity or discontinuity between the school and the home, in terms of participation structures, resource materials and culturally meaningful interactions. Literacy is also a construct which exists in relation to structures of power in society. For families who have access to power, this is not a problem. For disempowered families, particularly of minority group status, the unchallenged power structure may deny them academic success. An important aspect of these relations of power is the affirmation or denial of the individual's cultural identity in the process of literacy learning. Chapter Two focuses on the important role of parents in supporting their children's school-related literacy learning.

2
LITERACY AT HOME AND SCHOOL

Introduction

This chapter focuses on parental involvement in children's reading. It explores the role of parents in directly supporting children's reading, and reviews studies which have identified gains in children's reading attainment through support at home. However, 'parental involvement in children's learning' does not have a universally agreed meaning.

What is 'parental involvement in children's learning'?

My use of the term 'parent' does not imply that all children live in the same household as their natal parents, or that the adults in a family are the sole contributors to young children's home literacy development. 'Parent' is used as shorthand for the main adult carer(s) in the household.

The involvement of parents in their children's schooling in Britain gained ground in educational thinking and policy-making during the 1980s and 1990s. From a base of very little visible involvement in schooling, parents are now invited to sit on school governing bodies, to become members of Parent Teacher Associations, to attend parents' evenings and annual general meetings, and to support children's learning both in school and at home. Parents now have the right to be consulted as part of the process of school inspection. The devolution of management of schools to governing bodies created an opportunity for parents to have a greater say in the running of their children's schools. However, the evidence is that these reforms have had little effect in empowering minority or working-class parents. Power is still largely in the hands of those articulate, middle-class parents who offer their services as school governors, rather than empowering the parent body as a whole (Golby, 1993; Blackledge, 1995).

Jowett and Baginsky (1991) conducted a questionnaire survey of all local education authorities in England and Wales, which asked questions about practices to involve parents in children's education. Responses demonstrated that there was considerable diversity of practice in the involvement of parents in their children's schooling. These ranged from parents painting classroom walls to sitting on the Education Committee with full voting rights; from attending English as a Second Language classes to assisting with school trips. However, the study did not report the *scale* of parental involvement in these activities. Where a local education authority reported that its schools were supported by parents working voluntarily in classrooms, this may have meant one or two parents in each school of several hundred children. Indeed Stierer (1985) conducted a study which showed that where parents helped teachers in classrooms, the average proportion of parents per class was 2.5 per cent. Wolfendale (1992) provides an overview of some of the areas of development in the involvement of parents in schooling during the 1970s and 1980s in Britain, as follows: parents coming into school to work alongside teachers; parents as educators at home; links between school and home, including written communication and home visits; community education; parents as governors; involvement in assessment of special educational needs; parental representation on local and national bodies. Many of these aspects of parental involvement in their children's schooling overlap. Communication between school and home is essential if progress is to be made in other areas.

Does parental involvement in reading lead to gains in children's literacy?

Tizard and Hughes (1984) studied children's spoken language interactions in preschool children at home and school. They fitted radio transmitter microphones to thirty girls of about four years of age and transcribed the recordings. The children were recorded at nursery school or class in the morning, and at home with their mothers in the afternoon. They found that the children's spoken language in the home was characterised by questioning, depth and variety. These features were largely missing from the nursery-school based interactions, as teachers had little time to spend talking with individual children. Although these were spoken interactions in general rather than specifically literacy interactions, both in nursery and at home the longest recorded conversations concerned books which the adult was reading aloud or had just read aloud.

Wells (1987) studied the language development of preschool children in Bristol. Over more than two years he used radiomicrophones to sample the naturally occurring conversation of young children. Wells identified aspects of conversation which appeared to be related to later attainment in school and particularly literacy related activities. One of the most important features found in the homes of children whose reading attainment could have been predicted was the sharing of stories which, he suggests, may be more important in literacy development than early introduction to features of print. Like Tizard and Hughes, Wells found that many children were engaged in richer conversations in the home with parents than in the classroom with teachers.

Parental involvement in children's reading and social class

A number of studies (Teale, 1986; Auerbach, 1989; Delgado-Gaitan, 1990) have demonstrated that young children participate in or observe a range of literacy activities in the home as part of daily living. Most children live in a family environment where the social process of literacy includes television listings, letter writing, shopping lists, newspapers, paying bills and many other reading and writing activities. Taylor (1983) reports a study which investigated the early reading behaviours of children from middle-class homes in New York State. Literacy was a functional set of activities for these children, whose parents did not teach them formally but included them in, for example, reading recipes and writing shopping lists. Taylor and Dorsey-Gaines (1988) set out to investigate whether working-class homes provided similarly literacy-rich environments. They found that in the homes of children of low socioeconomic status, parents were interested in studying, and that reading for information and pleasure was important. Children were often engaged in a variety of reading and writing activities, which were encouraged and valued by parents. Anderson and Stokes (1984) found that working-class children experienced a range of reading and writing opportunities, including literacy events for daily living needs (e.g. filling in forms to obtain welfare benefits), entertainment (e.g. solving a crossword puzzle) and religion (e.g. Bible-reading sessions). In Teale's (1986) study preschool children from minority, low-income groups were also engaged in home literacy activity.

In the National Child Development Study (Davie, Butler and Goldstein, 1972) all the children born in one week in 1958 in Britain – over 15000 – were followed through from birth. When they were 7 their reading attainment was tested. The thirty per cent of children who achieved relatively poorly on the test were studied more closely. It was found that the incidence of poor readers was related to a number of home factors, especially social class. Children of fathers who were semi-skilled manual workers were more than twice as likely to be poor readers than were those whose fathers were in professional/technical jobs. In another study Hannon and McNally (1986) compared the reading test scores of middle-class and working-class 7-year-olds and found a 27-point difference in mean scores – equivalent to more than two years' development. An earlier study in Nottingham (Newson and Newson, 1977) found that twice as many working-class parents of seven-year-olds reported that their children were non-readers as did middle-class parents. The evidence suggests, then, that reading attainment is strongly related to social class, at least when it is measured by reading tests.

If children of low socio-economic status families perform less well in reading tests at school, it is worth considering what factors might affect this difference. Wells (1985) found that there were considerable differences in the number of books available to children at home. Some children were read as many as four stories per day, while others were not read to at all. Wells concluded that some children would have experienced around 6000 reading interactions by the age of five, while others experienced very few, if any. The best predictor of overall academic achievement at age 7 for these children was a test of their knowledge of literacy. The children who scored well on this test were those whose parents read more, owned more books, and read more often with their children. Adams (1990) found that in the United States a typical middle-class child enters school with between 1000 and 1700 hours of one-to-one book reading interactions, while a child from a low socio-economic status family averages about 25 hours. McCormick and Mason (1986) demonstrated differences in the availability and use of books in homes of different socio-economic status. Forty-seven per cent of working-class parents reported having no alphabet books at home, compared with three per cent of professional parents. Feitelson and Goldstein (1986) found that 61 per cent of preschool children of working-class did not own a single book, whereas preschool children of middle-class owned an average of 54 books. The same study revealed that 96 per cent of the children of middle-class homes were read to daily, whereas 61 per cent of the children of lower-class homes were not read to at all. So there seems to be some correlation between the number of reading books available to children in the home, and their later academic achievement. This is not to say that there is a simple process of cause and effect; there are many other factors which influence children's reading attainment.

Many parents report that they try to help their children with literacy learning. One study compared parents' and teachers' perspectives on early literacy development (Hannon and James, 1990). They found that not only were parents interested in preschool literacy, but that they claimed to spend time engaged in reading and writing activities with their children. Farquhar, Blatchford, Plewis and Tizard (1985) interviewed the parents of over 200 Reception class children and found that they involved themselves in children's school learning, including literacy. In the Newson and Newson (1977) study researchers found that over 80 per cent of parents of 7-year-olds from every social class claimed to have given their children help with reading at some time. But this willingness to help was too often mischannelled for lack of advice, encouragement and appreciation from teachers. The Bullock Report (DES, 1975) made the ground-breaking assertion that that there was no doubt of the value of parents' involvement in the early stages of reading. What needed careful thought was the nature of that involvement.

Hewison and Tizard (1980) conducted a study of 7-year-old children, all from working-class families in Dagenham. They recognised that it was easy to overlook the fact that in spite of the general trend outlined above, many working-class children *do* become good readers. They asked what it was about these children or their home backgrounds that facilitated this, and investigated what aspects of parents' day-to-day activities with their children had the greatest impact on reading attainment. They looked at factors such as parents' attitudes to children's play and discipline, whether there was much conversation with the child, whether stories were read to them, how the children spent their leisure time, what attitudes parents had towards school, and so on. They also looked at mothers' language behaviour and at children's IQ scores. While very few parents had consulted the school about helping their child with reading, and none said the school encouraged them to do this, half of the parents regularly heard their child read at age 7. Hewison and Tizard concluded that parental help with reading had a significant impact on reading attainment.

Following the Hewison and Tizard (1980) study, a number of researchers set out to discover the robustness of the finding that parental involvement with children's reading had a significant effect in producing literacy gains. These studies almost exclusively investigated home reading support of school-related literacy. That is, the studies focused on parents supporting children with school reading books. They are now discussed.

Hearing children read

Hannon, Jackson and Weinberger (1986) studied how 52 working-class children, aged 5-7, were heard to read in school by their class teachers and at home by their parents. Previous studies (Gulliver, 1979; Campbell, 1981) had investigated how teachers hear children read, but there was no comparable study of parents hearing their children read. The Hewison and Tizard (1980) study had reported on *what* parents did with their children, but not *how* they did it. Hannon *et al*'s (1986) study provided a close-up view of parents and teachers hearing children read. Tape recordings were made of children reading at home and at school. School reading sessions tended to be shorter than those at home, and more subject to interruptions. Recordings were analysed in terms of the 'moves', that is the interventions in the reading process made by the adults involved. A descriptive system of 21 categories of moves was applied to 104 sessions, and 3600 moves were identified. The teacher's or parent's strategy in hearing reading was defined as the proportion of moves in different categories. The study found that there were significant similarities between the parents' and teachers' strategies in hearing children read. There were similarities in the range of moves made, and the relative importance given to the different kinds of moves. Teachers and parents both used moves which were concerned with running the reading session, and both groups frequently told the child the next word in the text where there was a hesitation. There were also differences, however: teachers praised children more often, and teachers were more concerned to provide a reading model, and to establish the meaning of the text, than were parents. Parents asked children to use phonic strategies more often, while teachers were more concerned with children's understanding of the text.

Hannon *et al* (1986) began their examination of parents' and teachers' reading support strategies by distinguishing moves made in response to children's miscues from those made at other points in a reading session. When children did not read accurately, there were several ways in which adults responded, such as telling the child by one means or another that a mistake had been made. One of the most common responses was to simply *provide the word (or phrase)* that the child needed. Or the adult might pause to allow a child the opportunity to work it out alone. The study found that responses to miscues were a larger proportion of the parent moves (about two thirds) than of the teacher moves (about half). In other words, parents were more likely to wait until a child was in difficulty before making a move, whereas teachers were more likely to take the initiative at other times. However, when their response to miscues was examined, it was found that teachers' and parents' strategies were not very different. For example, on about fifty per cent of occasions both groups provided children with words or phrases. Even where there was a statistically significant difference in the use of other moves, the moves made by parents and teachers were relatively similar. It is widely accepted in the teaching of reading that children should be encouraged to attend to the meaning of what they read, and to use their understanding to overcome reading difficulties. Conscious of teachers' worries that parents might teach children to read 'parrot fashion' or to simply memorise text, the study looked for any identifiable lack of concern for children's understanding. Overall, the researchers concluded that parents showed virtually the same concern for understanding as did teachers. For the parents, however, the concern was restricted mainly to occasions when they had to respond to a child's difficulties, whereas teachers were more active in also trying to promote understanding at other points in a reading session. The implications for practice from this study seem to be that there are no grounds for considering that parents as a group are not capable of teaching their children to read by listening to them read at home.

Hannon *et al* (1986) concluded that there was considerable similarity in the range of moves used by teachers and parents, and in the proportion of moves made within categories. However, their report made little of the fact that the investigation was conducted as part of the Belfield Project (Hannon, 1987), an intervention project which was specifically set up to increase parents' ability to support their children's reading at home. Parents received home visits, reading cards and a printed advice sheet of how to hear children read. One of the instructions on the advice sheet, for example, was that parents should smooth out difficulties by telling children words they didn't know. This may invalidate the finding of Hannon *et al* that one of the chief similarities between teacher and parent strategies was telling children words they didn't know. It may be that parents were following instructions rather than using their usual support strategies. Notwithstanding this, the lasting contribution of the Hannon *et al* study is to provide a descriptive scheme with which to analyse reading interactions at home and at school.

The Haringey Project

In pursuing the results of the Dagenham study referred to earlier (Hewison and Tizard, 1980), Tizard, Schofield and Hewison (1982) conducted a study in Haringey, London, to test the hypothesis that increasing parental involvement in hearing children read at home would increase children's performance on standardised reading tests. A collaboration between teachers and parents was organised so that every child in two randomly chosen top infant classes at two schools was regularly heard reading at home from books sent by the class teacher. The intervention was continued for two years. Comparison was made with the parallel classes at the same schools, and with randomly chosen classes at two schools where children were given extra reading tuition in school.

The study showed a highly significant improvement by children who received extra practice at home in comparison with control groups, but no comparable improvement by children who received extra help at school. The gains were made consistently by children of all ability levels. Parents were not given special training in how to hear their children read but, after an initial talk which was based in the school or home, all agreed to allow a researcher to visit them at home two or three times each term to hear the child reading to them. During home visits it was the practice of the researchers to offer the parents advice. The study concluded that children who received parental help made significantly greater reading attainment gains than comparable children who did not. The Haringey Project, as it became known, was influential in persuading schools to adopt the practice of sending children home with school reading books.

Of particular interest here is the fact that Tizard *et al* reported that the study was carried out in 'multiracial' schools and communities, although they did not specify which linguistic groups were involved, how many were minority group families, or how many of the parents involved were unable to read, write, speak or comprehend English. One of the conclusions drawn by the researchers was that in 'multiracial' schools it is feasible and practicable to involve nearly all parents in formal, school-focused educational activities with their children, even if the parents are non-literate and/or largely non-English speaking. What is missing from the data presented in the Haringey study is any clear picture of precisely *how* non-literate, non-English speaking parents contributed to children's reading. The support may have been offered by older, literate siblings; or it may be that the parents provided a relatively passive, yet supportive audience. Certainly the latter is implied in the study's conclusions:

> the fact that some children read to parents who could not themselves read English, or in a few cases cannot read at all, did not prevent improvement in the reading skills of those children, or detract from the willingness of the parent to collaborate with the school. (Tizard *et al*, 1982, p14)

Although the results of the Haringey Project sent a message throughout the educational community that reading at home was a significant contributor to children's school literacy learning, it was still not clear by what mechanisms the literacy gains were brought about (Hewison, 1985). When Hewison (1988a) conducted a follow-up study, testing the same children three years after the end of the intervention, the beneficial effects of the project were still apparent. At 11, children who had been participants in the parent involvement exercise were not just reading better than local controls but in some respects their performance also compared favourably with national standards. Again, Hewison was unable to say why these gains occurred. She speculates that the supportive home visits may have had the effect of both offering practical advice and maintaining motivation, so that parents developed a clear idea of which specific reading support strategies were likely to be effective. Elsewhere Hewison (1988b) speculates that the crucial factor in the success of the Haringey Project was giving the children opportunity for extra reading practice in a motivating context. She acknowledges, though, that further research was required to identify key components in the project's success. Cummins (1996) speculates that many of the children in the Haringey study would have translated or paraphrased the story for their parent in their home language if their knowledge of English was limited. Cummins suggests that this constitutes a cognitively demanding activity that may have increased the children's overall ability to analyse the semantic and syntactic aspects of text. Again, in the absence of hard data to this effect, this is speculation. It does, however, suggest a direction for further research.

The Belfield Project

A number of studies later attempted to substantiate Tizard *et al*'s findings, by setting up and evaluating similar reading-at-home projects. The most extensive was the study which became known as the Belfield Project (Hannon, 1987), conducted over five years in a primary school in a Social Priority Area in the north of England. Although there had previously been no attempt to ensure that all children regularly took home reading books, the school had tried hard for some years to work closely with parents in teaching reading. Following the methods employed by the Haringey Project, children were encouraged to take their reading books home daily and parents were encouraged to hear them read at home. Advice and support for parents was provided through parents' meetings, informal parent-teacher contacts, handouts of suggestions, and home visiting. Although there was already a substantial amount of parental involvement in their children's reading before the project, by the end of the five years this was doubled. Standardised reading tests were used to compare the reading attainment of children in the project with children in previous cohorts who had passed through the school before there had been this special intervention to involve parents. Reading test data indicated that the Project had only a slightly positive impact on children's reading test performance.

The Hannon (1987) study confirmed the findings of Hewison and Tizard (1980), that many working-class parents regularly hear their children read at home in the infant years, and that this is strongly associated with children's reading test attainment. However, at the end of three years in the Belfield Project the children's mean reading test scores remained firmly within the usual range for working-class samples; the gains of the Haringey Project had not been repeated. Hannon (1987) suggests that the differences between the results of the Haringey and Belfield Projects may be accounted for in several ways. Firstly, the extent and nature of the home visiting in the Belfield Project may have been less helpful to parents than that in the Haringey Project, which used outside researchers with time and specialist expertise – but this cause is speculative as there are no comparative data. Secondly, it may be that the extent of parental involvement going on before the Project period meant that differences were not as great as in the Haringey Project (Hannon, Jackson and Weinberger, 1986). This does raise the question, however, of why reading test scores of children in the Belfield study were well below the national norm both before and after the project. Thirdly, Hannon suggests that the 'multiracial' character of the Haringey schools meant that the intervention may have had much more impact than the Belfield Project, in a largely white, working-class area. This third explanation is also speculative but it has some important implications: if a reading-at-home intervention has a greater impact on minority language families this might be because they are so often excluded by schools.

In a separate report, Hannon (1986) presents qualitative data which demonstrate positive outcomes of the Belfield Project. One finding to emerge very clearly was that almost all parents welcomed the opportunity to be involved in teaching their children to read. Also, the teachers involved in the project generally said that their impression was that the children's attitude to reading had changed: they were reading with greater enthusiasm, and reading more books. Hannon concludes that it is entirely feasible to involve working-class parents in their children's reading over several years. Several other, smaller-scale studies have been documented, once again with equivocal results. Studies by Bloom (1987) and Ashton and Jackson (1986) failed to achieve the effects of the Haringey study but a number of shorter studies have recorded gains in children's reading test scores (Lindsay, Evans and Jones, 1985; Leach and Siddall, 1990; Burdett, 1986). Hannon (1995) suggests that a crucial factor in the varying results of these studies may be the duration of the reading projects: where gains in children's reading attainment were found, studies were generally of shorter duration than the Belfield Project. However, this theory does not account for Hewison's (1988a) finding that the beneficial effects of the Haringey Project had not washed out by age eleven.

Specific approaches to parental involvement in children's reading

The research reviewed so far has suggested that parents can play an important role in their children's literacy learning. However, for reasons which are not clear, the pattern of literacy gains is inconsistent from project to project. There is some evidence (Toomey, 1993) that parents are able to make the most valuable input to their children's literacy progress when they are equipped with clear strategies for intervention in reading with their children. It is this view that underpins initiatives which prescribe a more specific, precise involvement than hitherto seen in the 'open' approaches reviewed above.

Paired Reading

'Paired Reading' is one of the most widespread specific approaches to involving parents in their children's reading. The technique relies on a structured interaction between a reading tutor and tutee (Topping, 1992a). It is distinctive in that the child chooses the text to be read, as long as it falls within an appropriate readability level, otherwise the tutor may offer guidance. Tutor and tutee begin reading together, and where the tutee makes an error, the tutor repeats the word until the tutee reads it correctly. When the tutee is confident to try reading alone, he or she makes a pre-arranged non-verbal signal to tell the tutor to stop reading. The tutee then reads alone until making an error and not correcting it within five seconds, when the same correction procedure is applied, and the pair revert to reading together. There is emphasis throughout on praise for correct reading and self-correction. Families generally contract into the scheme for five sessions a week of at least five minutes, during an initial intensive period of eight to nine weeks. Reviews of the effectiveness of Paired Reading projects have been provided by Topping and Lindsay (1992) and Topping (1996). In the studies reviewed, involving over a thousand children, for each month passed the average Paired Reader gained

4.2 months in reading age for accuracy and 5.4 months for comprehension. Follow-up data suggested that the benefits of the interventions did not 'wash out' with time, although there was a deceleration of progress after the initial intervention period (Topping, 1992a). However, trialling the intervention in a number of schools (in Kirklees LEA) meant that it was difficult to ensure consistency of approach. It was not known precisely how parents carried out the prescribed technique after the initial intensive period. Some of the participants may have reverted at times to a more relaxed, 'book sharing' approach. Also, follow-up measures were administered inconsistently: collection of follow-up data from the Kirklees study ranged from six to 82 weeks after the intervention period. A finding which was in line with some of the studies reviewed above was that home visiting by teachers was related to increased test scores.

Of particular relevance here is Topping's (1992b) report of the effect of the Kirklees Paired Reading Project on the 9.4 per cent of Asian participants. Reading test scores showed that at pre-test Asian participants were attaining less well than white participants, in both reading accuracy and comprehension. By post-test, the Asian participants had reduced the gap between themselves and the white participants in reading accuracy, but had fallen further behind white participants in comprehension. Nevertheless, their gain in accuracy was well above the rate of gain of non-participant white control group children, while similar to them in comprehension. Topping expresses reservations about the cultural and linguistic relevance of the reading tests used. Also, there was no check on whether the sample of Asian parents was in any way representative. Notwithstanding these reservations, he suggests that South Asian families tend to be preoccupied with reading accuracy at the expense of comprehension. Jungnitz (1985) reports a study of ten Asian families of Year 3/Year 4 children who were supported in the use of Paired Reading techniques. Most of the parents could not act as reading tutors because they were not proficient in written or spoken English, so in most cases siblings became the tutors. After supportive home visits the project group made better than usual gains in reading comprehension test scores. The control group received less support than the experimental group, however, so direct comparison was not possible. Topping (1992b) also provides a descriptive report of Paired Reading projects which 'operated successfully' (p23) in

Kirklees schools with 100% Asian pupils. He concludes that Paired Reading with minority language children is possible, effective and feasible.

Pause, Prompt, Praise

A second specific home reading intervention, known as Pause, Prompt, Praise (PPP), was developed in New Zealand as a means of offering additional support to older low-attaining readers. The initial research work involved observation and training in home settings with a group of 10- to 12-year-old children and their parents, and resulted in the production of a parent training package. The strategy was developed as a consequence of finding that when listening to their children read at home parents did not generally pause after an error before correcting it for the child, so denying the opportunity for self-correction. PPP was designed for use in dyadic reading interactions so that low attaining readers could have more opportunities to self-correct errors and to practise problem-solving strategies (Glynn, 1996).

Helping readers to use these strategies required tutors to learn to implement a set of specific tutoring skills. PPP tutoring involves first *pausing* when a reader makes an error, to allow the reader to self-correct. When the error is not self-corrected, tutors offer different types of prompt to assist the reader with the meaning of the word or with other decoding strategies (e.g phonic). Tutors offer *praise* when readers use independent strategies such as self-correction. Glynn and McNaughton (1985) reviewed twelve PPP studies, which showed strong gains in children's reading test scores: increases of as much as 11 months per month of trained tutoring. However, all of these studies were of older, low-attaining readers. Further studies with children who were average or slightly below average attaining readers showed that they made no greater gains than control groups given untrained tutoring.

Of particular interest here is the PPP work carried out with minority language families. Glynn and Glynn (1986) found that five Khmer-speaking mothers of 6- to 7-year-old migrant children were able to improve their children's rate of reading progress at school more than the school programme alone, even though the mothers knew only a few words of English and had received little or no schooling in Cambodia. In this study mothers and children worked together, using either Khmer or English to work out the meaning of the books sent home from school. The apparent success of this intervention is tempered by the fact that the PPP model was not strictly adhered to: the parents and children used a more 'open' approach to interpreting text, which Glynn and Glynn term 'Shared Reading'. The authors regretted that this study did not present data on the mother-child interaction processes which took place in the Shared Reading sessions. So we do not know how much mothers or children interrupted, prompted, supported or questioned each other, or initiated oral language interactions, nor to what extent these interactions occurred in Khmer or English. PPP has also been developed in the Maori language. Initial indications suggest that it is being implemented successfully (Glynn, 1996). PPP seems to offer great potential for sibling tutoring, possibly in dual languages (Topping, 1996).

Comparative studies

Leach and Siddall (1990) set up a comparison study in Western Australia which sought to establish whether Hearing Reading (based on the Haringey Project), Paired Reading or Pause, Prompt, Praise was the most effective intervention. The researchers also included a more prescriptive, 'Direct Instruction' programme, based on a phonic instructional package. Each of the groups of parents received some training, although the Hearing Reading (HR) group's information was in written form, whereas the Direct Instruction (DI) group received four and a half hours of face-to-face training and the PR and PPP parents one-and-a-half hours of training. Reading sessions were conducted by parents in their own homes for ten to fifteen minutes per weekday for ten weeks. Post-intervention reading test scores strongly indicated that the PR and DI groups made greater progress. There was not such strong support in the data for PPP or HR strategies, although the PPP children made greater gains than the HR group. The gains using the DI approach may have been due to the longer training. Although this may invalidate the study, it is an important finding in itself, as it suggests that parents may be more effective reading tutors when they have a clear and assured understanding of their role. As the PPP method attends to errors and allows for self-correction, there may be evidence here that teaching children to self-correct enhances their reading attainment. The success of the PR programme may support the thesis that parents are more successful tutors when they are sure of their role. This small-scale, short study (forty parents) should be treated with some caution; but it does suggest that parents benefit from explicit knowledge about how to teach their children to read.

Toomey (1993) reviewed the evidence of studies of parents hearing their children read and he notes that in a number of the studies of parental involvement in children's reading, home visits by researchers and/or teachers seemed to have a beneficial effect. This effect is borne out by a study of home reading in several local education authorities in Britain (Jowett and Baginsky, 1991). The relative rigour and frequency of home visits may account for some of the differences between the results of the Haringey and Belfield Projects (Hannon, 1987), and in Paired Reading projects home visiting improved test outcomes (Topping, 1995), which suggests that parents are more able to teach their children to read when they have been given comprehensible support. Toomey concludes that there appear to be good grounds for giving parents of low-competence readers some form of training but adds the caveat that a clear inference to be drawn from the relative success of parent training schemes is the in-advisability of giving parents advice without some means of determining their capacity to follow it, and its appropriateness to the needs of the parents and children concerned. Toomey calls for close observation studies of what goes on during parent-child reading episodes, as little is still known about what are the crucial variables in parental involvement in children's literacy learning.

Summary

The evidence from research studies is that there is no clear, simple answer to the question of how parents can most effectively help their children with their school reading at home. A range of studies shows that parents are willing to support their children, and that they want their children to learn to read. The studies reviewed here demonstrate the ways in which parents respond to school-related home reading tasks. While the evidence is inconsistent, taken together the studies suggest that effective parental support practices in home reading interactions include attention to the meaning of the text through discussion, offering support through reading together, and responding positively to errors in reading. Some of the research provides evidence that specific interventions, requiring of parents particular behaviours in hearing their children read, can benefit the children's literacy learning. These studies seem to demonstrate that it is important for parents to have a clear understanding of their role as home literacy tutors. Other studies suggest that parents respond to receiving books from school without requiring instruction about how to most effectively use them with their children. A number of studies focus on the meaning of the text, suggesting that it is parents' and children's talk about text that is the most important variable in home reading interactions.

In a review of home reading instruction practices, Francis (1987) suggests that Paired Reading is a constraining practice which may achieve its narrow objectives of increasing reading test scores but is unlikely to affect other important aspects of becoming literate, and may even have detrimental effects. She suggests that understanding and enjoyment of text are undeveloped in the practice. Francis makes the additional, important point that the mere distinction between home and school practices of hearing children read fails to engage with the evidence that all homes are different. Home literacy environments may differ more from each other than from the school. The school-advocated practice of parents hearing children read implies an extension of schooling into the home, at the expense of paying attention to the social process of literacy in the home. Literacy learning is never culturally neutral, and so no study of parents and children reading together can be viewed outside of its cultural context. Many of the studies reviewed in this chapter, however, fail to make explicit the cultural and linguistic backgrounds of the participants. Chapter Three focuses on studies which have investigated home reading interactions in specific cultural minority contexts.

3

PARENTAL INVOLVEMENT IN CHILDREN'S READING IN MULTILINGUAL CONTEXTS

Introduction

In this chapter I focus on the involvement in their children's literacy learning of parents who speak minority langauges. Literacy and literacies have different meanings among different cultural groups. Schools and other institutions often demand that minority language parents adopt the linguistic and cultural rules of the dominant group if they are to support their children's academic learning effectively, while often doing little to ensure that this can happen. Parent education programmes may actually increase educational inequality if they only reach the most easily accessible parents. Parents who do not speak, read or write the language of the dominant group are often among those who are seen least at the school.

Models of parental involvement in multilingual contexts

Research on parent involvement suggests that there are three broadly defined models that describe the nature and outcomes of parent involvement in children's schooling (Delgado-Gaitan, 1990). Involving parents can be viewed as the school's attempt to change home life to fit it for the values of the school, or as the parents' attempt to change the school (e.g. through participation in governing bodies and other committees), or as a genuinely collaborative process in which both school and parents benefit from their relationship. In the first model, schools try to improve the family's competence in helping their children learn and providing the type of home learning environment that accentuates the positive elements of cognitive and emotional factors. This model may assume a deficit view of some parents and imply that there is an agreed body of information which all parents need in order to bring up their children properly. Some parents have this knowledge, while others do not and need to acquire it from teachers. The model assumes that home activities are insufficient to meet the school's demands for helping children to achieve and that this can be corrected by school-designed interventions that make home socialisation compatible with the school culture.

In the second model, parents may try to change the schools to make them more responsive to parents, in the hope that if educators become more attuned to the family and the culture of the home, they can teach and serve the child more effectively. Accordingly, parent involvement means parents participating in the classroom and school, as well as on policy or advisory groups. The parents learn to deal with schools, and the goal is to change the institution and make it more responsive to student and family needs, so giving children greater educational advantage. The assumption is that the school will accommodate the parents' suggestions and influence.

The third model assumes that factors in the home, school and community are interrelated and that cooperation exists between the family and school. So parent education needs to be concerned not only with how to support children's learning but also with strategic issues of how parent involvement fits into the larger social scheme, including the parents' employment opportunities and their social position. Delgado-Gaitan's summary reminds us that parental involvement in children's schooling is not a unitary, homogeneous development but will probably be different in different communities.

Parental involvement may promote collaborative relations of power by empowering parents in, for example, the process of policy-making. On the other hand, well-meaning school initiatives to involve parents in schooling may obstruct some parents' access to empowerment, if they can only do the bidding of the school staff or if they encounter structures that encourage only certain parents to participate. Parent involvement is therefore more than a discrete set of activities that teach a specific skill. For Delgado-Gaitan (1990), the most important skills which the schools need to help parents acquire are those of social competence and social literacy – concepts which extend beyond discrete tasks. It is important to consider the need for parents to work collectively with each other and the school so that they learn the meaning of parent involvement by becoming literate about the culture of the school, the classroom curriculum and how resources are accessed. And the school needs to learn about the families it serves. The more the school recognises and values the children's home culture in its curriculum and its communication with parents, the more effective home-school communication will be. This model presumes a highly interactive context between parents and children, teachers and students, teachers and parents, and parents and parents. Through collective effort parents can learn to act as advocates for their children beyond the homework level and provide their children with appropriate resources as they move through their schooling even if the home language and culture differ from that of the school. An interactive context between teachers and parents may be achieved when parents possess the cultural resources to gain access to the school.

Cultural capital in parental involvement

The notion of *cultural capital*, developed by Bourdieu (Bourdieu, 1977; Bourdieu and Passeron, 1977) in a majority language context, can provide a useful model in understanding relations of power in home-school inter-actions in minority language settings. Bourdieu argues that schools draw unevenly on the social and cultural resources of a society. Schools use particular linguistic structures, authority patterns and learning models; children from higher social locations enter schools already familiar with these patterns. The cultural experiences of the home facilitate children's adjustment to school, thereby transforming cultural resources into cultural capital. Although Bourdieu does not examine parental involvement in children's schooling, his model points to the importance of relations of power between classes and cultures in facilitating or impeding parents' negotiation of the process of schooling. In Bourdieu's terms, the culture of the school is a creation of the dominant culture. It tends to be similar to the culture of the dominant majority group in society. This limits the educational opportunities of children from non-dominant groups because the school demands competence in the dominant language and culture, and this is achieved through family background. Bourdieu argues that while the cultural capital that is valued in schools is not equally available to children or parents from different backgrounds, schools still operate as if all families had equal access to it.

Interpreting Bourdieu's model in the context of a study of parental involvement in schooling in white working-class and middle-class communities in the United States, Lareau (1987; 1989) suggests that cultural capital can provide a conceptual bridge between macro and micro levels of analysis, a link between the actual practices of parental involvement and their relation to structures of power in society. Lareau's critique notes that while Bourdieu conceives of cultural capital as the process through which individuals gain access to structures of power in schooling (and elsewhere), the empirical evidence which demonstrates what individuals do to achieve this in their microinteractions with schools is unclear. Also, individuals within a social class or culture differ from each other. Several individuals may possess cultural resources but may use these resources differently (or not at all) to gain educational advantage. There is a need for further studies which analyse the microinteractions by which parents attempt to gain access to structures of power in schooling. Lareau (1989) proposes that in the context of home-school relations it is necessary to posit a three-part process: (i) the possession of cultural capital (ii) the activation and investment of these cultural resources, and (iii) the attainment of social profit from these investments. She calls for studies which investigate how the cultural resources of some groups may be more likely than those of others to be profitably activated in the home-school setting. Lareau's research (1987) found that in the working-class school (Colton) in her study, parents turned over education to the teachers; in the middle-class school (Prescott) parents saw education as a shared enterprise and monitored and supported their children's progress. When asked to read to their children, Colton parents were reluctant because they felt that their educational skills were inadequate; Prescott parents, however, were confident about doing so. Colton parents were dependent on teachers and felt that they had few rights in the process of schooling; Prescott parents felt that they had the right and a responsibility to raise issues of their choosing and even to criticise teachers. This study highlights the need for more extensive research in relations of power and cultural capital in educational settings.

Corson (1993) adapts Bourdieu's model in developing a theory of language and power in minority language school settings and refutes misreadings (Apple, 1982; Aronowitz, 1981) of Bourdieu which assume that cultural and linguistic capital is exclusively the preserve of dominant groups. On the contrary, Bourdieu's central point is that all groups possess cultural and linguistic capital of their own, but not necessarily the same form of capital that is recognised and valued in education. Corson makes the point that by moving from one cultural context to another, power relationships change, as does cultural capital. This point is salient: it is too easy to interpret minority-language parents' invisibility in the school setting as being due to a 'lack' of cultural capital. In fact if minority-language parents are apparently disempowered in terms of their access to their children's schooling, this is due not to a *lack* of cultural or linguistic capital but to their cultural and linguistic capital, however useful in their own community context, being different from the cultural resources required by the school.

Literacy and empowerment through parental involvement

minority-culture parents living in poor socioeconomic conditions often face isolation from the school culture, which can lead to a breakdown in communication between parents and school. Schools facilitate the exclusion of parents by demanding of them activities which require specific majority culturally based knowledge and behaviours about the school as an institution (Delgado-Gaitan, 1991). From research in the Spanish-speaking community in California, Delgado-Gaitan concludes that parent involvement in children's literacy learning can become a process of empowerment. She characterised empowerment as a process centred in the local community and involving mutual respect, critical reflection, caring and group participation, through which people lacking an equal share of resources gain greater access to and control over these resources. In the empowerment process people change so that they are able to determine their choices and goals. This is a somewhat different conception of literacy from that measured by gains in reading test scores; however, it is one which is consistent with that developed by Freire (1970) and Cummins (1994a).

Lankshear (1997) counsels against the trivialisation of the term 'empowerment', which may become meaningless if overused. Lankshear insists that studies which make claims about empowerment should identify: the *subject* of empowerment; the *structures* in relation to which a person may be empowered (or disempowered); the *processes* through which empowerment (or disempowerment) occurs; and the *outcomes* which result from being thus empowered (or disempowered). Lankshear points out that a powerful literacy is a particular use of literacy, and not literacy skills themselves.

Delgado-Gaitan's (1990) study focused on 20 Spanish-speaking second and third grade children from one school and their families. All the parents were immigrants from Mexico, and of low socioeconomic status. The context of the study was the reading interaction between parent and child. The parents' knowledge about text and their ability to help their children to make the link between home and school literacy activities constituted the crucial relationship between literacy activities in home and classroom. The twenty children were observed reading at home with parents and in school with teachers, and parents and teachers were interviewed by researchers about the role of the parents in children's literacy learning. The study was based on the premise that to the extent that parents can interpret classroom text that goes home and guide their children in dealing with it, they support their children emotionally, cognitively and linguistically. Classroom-based observations of reading provided points of comparison between home and school literacy activity.

The home literacy activities data showed that most parents faced difficult problems in supporting their children's reading because they lacked information about the school's expectations of them and the skills to provide maximum support with school books. Parents provided their children with a range of non-school learning contexts in the home but parents with minimal Spanish and English literacy expressed feelings of constraint in their ability to perform school-related literacy activities with their children. Although they valued their children's schooling and expressed great desire to have their children succeed in school, they only had vague notions about how to help them learn. Most parent-child interaction about text took place in Spanish because of the parents' limited proficiency in English. On rare occasions, the children read to their parents in English and, depending on the parents' facility with English, they directly assisted in the reading process. But many felt inadequate about supporting their children's schoolwork if they had to read in English. Examination of home literacy tasks created an opportunity to understand the parents' role in their children's schooling. The majority of parents felt confused about homework activities because school expectations seemed unclear. Feelings of incompetence at helping their children perpetuated a sense of isolation among the families and both groups expressed their helplessness as educators of their own children. When school literacy activities are imported into the home without explicit support, families may be unable to participate in their children's learning. Teacher interviews revealed that teachers had little or no knowledge of the home language and literacy environments of the families, so made inappropriate recommendations and held unrealistic expectations of families, which in turn caused increased frustration from all sides. These parents and teachers were in agreement about the potential efficacy of parental involvement in children's reading but could not bring about change or achieve their goals. The parents were denied access to structures of power in their children's schooling because their literacy did not fit with the expectations of the school.

Teachers' attitudes and practices in involving minority language parents in their children's reading

Teachers' perceptions of the process of involving parents in their children's learning may be different from the perceptions of the parents themselves. This section reviews research studies which have identified teachers' attitudes to the contribution made by minority language parents to their children's learning, and studies which have investigated what teachers do to involve minority language parents in their children's reading at home.

Becker and Epstein (1982) conducted a questionnaire survey of 3,700 teachers in USA to identify their practices for involving parents in their children's learning at home. Virtually all teachers reported that they talked with children's parents, sent notices home and had discussions with them at parents' evenings. Most teachers said that they discussed with all parents how they taught reading in the classroom, but some did so in reality with only a few parents. The teachers' responses suggested that many of them believed that parent involvement at home could be an important contributor to children's learning yet few had any idea how to initiate parental involvement. Teacher opinion was divided about whether parents had sufficient skills to teach their children to read at home but two-thirds of the teachers said that they asked parents to read to their children or listen to their children read, and more than one fifth named this activity as the most valuable parent-involvement technique. It was clear that some teachers of students from less educated families had developed techniques that enabled these parents to participate in the schooling of their children and to co-operate effectively with the school.

In Dauber and Epstein's (1993) study of low socioeconomic status communities in Baltimore, the strongest and most consistent predictors of parent involvement at school and at home were the specific teacher practices that encouraged and guided parent involvement. Regardless of parent education, family size, student ability or ethnicity, parents were more likely to become partners in their children's education if they perceived that the schools had clear strategies for involving parents at home on homework and reading activities. When parents believed that schools were doing little to involve them, they reported doing little at home. When parents perceived that the school was doing much to involve them, they did far more at home. So the school's practices and not just family characteristics affected the parents' level of involvement. Significantly, although teachers reported that most parents were not involved with their children's education, and did not want to be, these same parents told a different story, saying that they were involved with their children's education, but that they needed more and better information from teachers about how to help at home. Parents and teachers had very different perspectives about the role of parents in educating their children.

In Vincent's study of home-school relations in two urban school communities in Britain, where more than half of the families studied were of minority-cultures (Vincent, 1996), parents were often characterised by teachers as uninterested in their children's education. Some teachers said they welcomed parents reading at home with their children, but some expressed doubts about whether parents were using the 'correct' teaching methods. The teachers were reported to be unaware of many of the educational activities going on in families' homes. All teachers were united in their opposition to parents being involved in decision-making. In a study of parents' and teachers' attitudes to school-focused home book reading in New Zealand, McNaughton, Parr, Timperley and Robinson (1992) found most teachers supportive of the practice, as long as parents did not take too active a teaching role. However, the only instances in which teachers had ceased to send books home were where schools had high Maori and Pacific Island student populations. This finding supports research by Toomey (1989) that parental involvement in home-school reading can exacerbate educational inequality by only reaching the easily accessible parents who possibly require less support than those who are less visible at the school. Toomey provides evidence that parents who have infrequent contacts with schools tend to be less confident dealing with teachers and helping their children's reading development, tend to have lower-achieving children, do not receive as much help from school, and are perceived more negatively by teachers. If they fail to reach out to these families, schools may give most of their help to high-contact parents, who usually need it less. In a Californian study of parental involvement in children's schooling (Lareau, 1989), some teachers suggested that parents did not value education, but they were all in favour of parents reading with their children at home. They operated a Read-at-Home programme, and awarded children a free book for every eight hours they read at home. The school provided forms which children took home for their parents to sign, testifying that their children had either read a book themselves or had a book read to them.

Clearly then, many teachers are supportive of minority language parents helping their children's reading at home but do not always find it straight-forward to involve them to maximim effect. There is evidence of a mismatch between teachers' and parents' perception of parents' commitment to their children's education and teachers may know little about the extent or nature of learning activities in minority-culture homes. The children of parents who are not frequently visible or accessible to teachers may be disadvantaged by a programme of parental involvement in children's reading.

Minority parents' attitudes to involvement in their children's reading

What of the parents' attitudes to helping their children to read? Observation of the literacy interactions at home and school complete only half the picture. Also important is the parents' perception of schools' expectations of them as educators of their children. Dauber and Epstein (1993) report results of a questionnaire study of 'hard-to-reach' inner-city parents in Baltimore. 2317 parents (over 50 per cent) responded to the questionnaire, which suggests that parents who were least involved in literacy at home may have been among the non-respondents. Although over thirty per cent of those who did respond had not completed high school the questionnaire data indicated significant, positive effects of teachers' reported practices to guide parents in how to help their children with school work at home. Parents who had advice from teachers were more likely to support their children's school work at home. The specific guidance teachers gave parents in how to help at home increased the kinds of help parents said they gave, and the time they devoted to helping their children learn. Parents in all the schools were emphatic about wanting such advice from the school and teachers. Chavkin and Williams (1993) asked similar questions of 1,188 African-American and Hispanic parents and found that over ninety per cent of the respondents considered the role of the parent as home tutor to be important, showing clearly that parents were interested in supporting their children's education, whatever their ethnicity or status.

Gregory (1996a) presents more detailed interview data from a much smaller group of Bangladeshi parents in London. These parents consistently expressed their commitment to their children's English literacy learning, while also wanting their children to learn the community language, Bengali. They sent their children to the *madressa*, or community school, where they learned to read the Qur'an. A number of parents in Gregory's study commented that they felt unable to help their children with reading school books, so it was best left to the teacher. In another study of Bangladeshi families in London, Tomlinson and Hutchison (1991) found that less than half of the parents interviewed believed that they were competent to read English books sent home from school with their children. Their chief reasons were reported to be (i) their view that it was for teachers to teach their children to read and (ii) their poor proficiency in English. Tizard, Mortimore and Burchell (1988) concluded from their study that minority parents were frequently excluded from their children's education by teachers so it was hardly surprising that many were wary of approaching the school.

Vincent (1996) interviewed 95 parents from two inner-city schools, many of Bangladeshi origin and even more of other minority language backgrounds. The Bangladeshi parents in Vincent's study felt strongly that the ethos of their children's school was shaped by teachers with whom they shared no common ground. Parents cited as evidence that the school had only one Bengali-speaking member of staff, made no provision for Bengali classes, and had no books in Bengali. Parents often resorted to using their children as interpreters when trying to speak to teachers, which prevented them from speaking freely about their children's educational progress (Harman, 1994). The Bangladeshi parents in Vincent's study also pointed out that communication between school and home was hampered by the fact that letters were sent out in English only. All the Bangladeshi parents interviewed reported that they had no easy access to information about their children's school progress and that teachers did not follow up incidents of racial abuse and harassment in the school. Forty per cent of the parents interviewed by Vincent found visiting their children's school intimidating. Overall, more than two thirds of the parents in the study said that they wanted to become more closely involved with the school but felt unable to do so. Instead, they made alternative arrangements, working with the children at home without reference to the class teacher, and/or taking them to supplementary classes.

As part of a wider study, Jowett and Baginsky (1991) interviewed parents of Asian children in an urban middle-school. All but two reported that they wanted more guidance from teachers about how they should work with their children at home. The parents also said that they would like the school to provide homework for the children throughout the middle school years, yet over half of the families had received home visits from teachers which specifically focused on parental involvement in children's reading. These home visits were supported with a video outlining the school's approach to teaching reading, which parents found to be of value. Parents said that they had learnt how they could help their children, especially using home and community language strategies, even though the video was in English only.

Ghuman and Gallop (1981) interviewed Bangladeshi parents about their contribution to their children's schooling. These parents said that they could not provide much support for their children's education. Fathers had little time, as they were often working in the evening. They expressed a concern that they knew little about the British education system, so they could not help their children. Most of the mothers did not speak English so could not help their children with their school-related reading. A study (Sneddon, 1994) of fifty minority-language families in north east London found that there was rarely anyone other than a child available to interpret between teacher and parent and that parents' meetings organised by the school were often inflexible in their timing, making attendance difficult.

Sneddon (1993) also reports an intervention project with Bangladeshi mothers who had little contact with their children's school. A women's support group was set up, and the mothers were able to report that their children had been bullied and subjected to racist attacks, and that this had adversely affected the children's learning. A similar project initiated for the parents of Turkish-speaking children (Sneddon, 1997) found that parents were concerned about reading at home, the availability of extra English support for children who needed it in class, and the availability of Turkish classes in the community. These parents had not been able to articulate their concerns to the school before a bilingual, bicultural Turkish community education group intervened. In a further intervention project (Karran, 1997), researchers interviewed Kashmiri and Bangladeshi mothers in their home language about their perceptions of their children's schools and found views that children were given insufficient homework and that British school children seemed to 'play' rather than work. Karran asked parents why they were not involved with their children's schooling at the school. Most of the Kashmiri mothers said that this was due mainly to their lack of English proficiency and (as a consequence, perhaps) that other family members spoke on their behalf. The Bangladeshi mothers replied mostly that they had to work at home during the day. Lack of English proficiency was significant for more than a quarter of these parents.

Simich-Dudgeon (1993) makes the point that parental involvement is differently interpreted by parents from different ethnic and cultural backgrounds and some find parental involvement activities a new cultural concept that must be learned. Simich-Dudgeon suggests that rather than trying to impose school-based activities on families who may have to learn new skills or cannot meet the demands of the school, schools should build on culturally appropriate activities which are already familiar to the parents. This 'additive' (p192) model allows minority parents to build confidence in their ability to assist their children at home. Simich-Dudgeon reports a study of the Trinity-Arlington Project in Washington, DC which trained teachers in parent involvement techniques and trained parents to work with their children. Over 350 minority language students and their parents or other adult carers (and siblings) were involved in the project. The families were largely Spanish-speaking Central Americans and speakers of Khmer, Vietnamese and Lao. The Khmer-speaking households were all headed by women, fifty per cent of whom had never had any schooling. Parent self-assessment of their English skills indicated that over eighty per cent of all the adult carers spoke little or no English, and less than ten per cent reported having some English fluency and literacy skills. Students reported that they were supported in home literacy activities not only by their parent or guardian but also by siblings. This finding raises important issues about the role of minority language parents in children's learning, and the appropriateness of sibling intervention. Many of the parents reported that although they wanted to help their children do well at school, they could not do so because they could not understand the language or concepts being taught to them. The Trinity-Arlington project provided evidence of the benefits of minority language parent and family involvement in school-focused home reading activities but indicated that continued research is needed to establish ways to involve all parents successfully in the education of their children, whatever their literacies.

Thus a range of studies indicate that minority language parents are very much committed to their children's education and want particularly to contribute to their children's literacy learning. But unless schools introduce specific, culturally-appropriate interventions which provide them with strategies for supporting their children's reading, they frequently feel disempowered as home literacy tutors. Parents may feel that they do not have proficiency in English or knowledge of English school reading methods or they may regard the teaching of English literacy as the province of the school, so think it is not for them to interfere; they may see the teaching process as part of the majority culture, and something from which they are excluded both by teachers and by the inappropriate demands made of them by schools.

Minority-language parents' responses to school-focused home literacy activities

Minority-language parents clearly do not find it a straightforward matter to support their children's reading in school-related home literacy activities when teachers send home reading books. A number of studies have investigated what happens in family reading interactions when they try to read school books with their children, and these are now reviewed. They raise a number of questions about cultural congruency and empowerment in the process of home reading tuition.

Minns (1996) took a close look at the home reading interactions of five young children and their parents, two of whom spoke minority languages. Minns notes that sharing a book with a child is always a form of social interaction that involves cultural transmission of attitudes, values, beliefs and skills. Reading practices between parents and children are neither neutral nor universal. One of the children, Gurdeep, was recorded in reading sessions which showed his parents inhibiting any response to the text through verbal interaction. Even when Gurdeep tried to initiate discussion about the text and illustrations, his father did not pursue the conversation about the world of the story but preferred to correct individual words at the expense of allowing a flow of meaning. Minns concluded that this approach to reading tuition derived from Gurdeep's father's cultural inheritance. The other Panjabi child in the study, Geeta, did not read with her parents because they were too busy with their business but instead read with her sister. Their reading dyads were characterised by co-operation and correction, as Geeta's sister made every effort to teach her to read, and Geeta showed confidence during these interactions although Minns reported some frustration on the part of the sister.

Reviewing Minns' data, Gregory (1996a) observes that the reading approaches favoured by British schools (in as much as these are common) are not necessarily superior to those in any culture in which children are successfully learning to read. It cannot be assumed that teachers, children and their families enter school with the same sense of what literacy is or how it is learned.

Goldenberg, Reese and Gallimore (1992) reported case studies of Hispanic kindergartners, literacy activities prompted by the children's attendance at school in Los Angeles. In four experimental classrooms, teachers initiated the use of simple photocopied story booklets (*Libros*) in Spanish. They introduced the booklets briefly to parents, and then sent them home regularly for the children to read with their parents. Teachers in four control classrooms sent home materials consisting of packets of photocopied work sheets with decontextualised letters and syllables and a strong phonic focus. The homes of ten of the children (five receiving each type of material) were visited 118 times in total by Spanish-speaking fieldworkers, producing just under 219 hours of observation, and parents were asked what they thought of the reading materials sent by the school. Results of the study showed that the school was influential in providing opportunities for children to initiate literacy-related activities at home. The researchers' hypothesis was that the Libros would prompt verbal interactions between parents and their children and increased attention to the meaning of the text, while the decontextualised worksheets were expected to produce literacy events that included little verbal interaction but would focus on the shapes and sounds of letters. But it was found that in both the Libros and worksheet groups, the children's literacy experiences were characterised by repetition and lack of attention to print-meaning relationships. The most powerful factors influencing how the materials were used were inherent not in the materials themselves but in the parents' interpretations of and responses to teaching literacy to their children. The fieldworkers often observed a child beginning to read a Libro aloud, either alone or at the parent's request but generally the parent would shift the task from reading to correcting the child for each word not read as written. Whether children used the Libros or the control work sheets, the activity involved copy and repetition, either orally or in writing, and virtually no attention was paid to relationships between print and meaning. These data seemed to indicate that the parents viewed literacy as a skills-based practice.

Goldenberg *et al* suggest that influential in this model of home reading was the parents' view of the schooling process: their view that children learn to read in school by engaging in repetitive activities led them to construct literacy-learning events heavy with repetition and copying. If an activity was perceived as school-like, it was transformed into a copying-and-repetition task. When parents interacted with their children in activities not perceived as learning tasks, meaning and content became central to the interaction. Goldenberg *et al* conclude that there are two ways of addressing minority parents' 'views and assumptions about literacy learning' (p529) : either to educate parents to expand their views on literacy development or to forgo training per se and instead concentrate on building on what parents already know, believe and can do.

However, for these parents the picture may be more complex. Rather than holding definite 'views' about how to teach their children to read they may have been trying to meet the school's demand that they listen to their child read, using an approach to teaching based on uncertainty, folk theory, lack of confidence and disempowerment. In an environment where parents can approach teachers easily and where the channels of communication between home and school are open, it may be possible to involve parents in broader home reading practices *and* build on what parents already know, believe and can do. Instead of interpreting these data as parental behaviours which have to be corrected or cultural behaviours which should be left as they are, it may be more appropriate to take an empowerment perspective, identifying the home reading interaction as the threshold between majority-culture school and minority-culture home, and one at which relations of power between the two settings become visible.

Delgado-Gaitan (1994) proposes a model of the empowerment process in which empowerment takes place at the individual level by building self-esteem and self-confidence. At the family level empowerment occurs when barriers are removed or incentives provided in local settings. In literacy interactions parents have the opportunity to talk about the world of the text and the world beyond it, in ways which convey values, provide a view of society, and imbue their children with a sense that they are important enough to receive their parents' attention. However, in many of the studies considered in this chapter, minority parents' response to the school-focused home literacy interaction is characterised by low self-esteem, lack of confidence and a view that they are inadequate for the role of home literacy tutor. Parents' response to the task of helping their child to read a school book may be reflected in their response to dominant cultural groups which emphasise a narrow conception of literacy, and regard minority language groups as inarticulate and illiterate.

The notion of empowerment, self-identity and self-esteem informed a study reported by Ada (1988), of a discussion-oriented project on children's literature designed around Spanish-speaking parents in Pajaro Valley, California. In monthly group meetings at which children's reading books in Spanish were discussed before being taken home to use with children, Ada attempted to teach parents how to use a 'creative reading' methodology. This required parents to ask questions about the text in a range of categories which framed the interaction between adults and children: descriptive, personal interpretive, critical and creative. In the descriptive phase factual recall was solicited; in the personal interpretive phase children were asked to respond to the text in terms of their own experience; critical questions asked children to make a critical analysis of the events and ideas of the story; and creative questions made readers think about how they would resolve similar questions to those in the story. Ada found that Spanish-speaking children and their parents gained confidence and self-esteem in the reading process; they joined the library and asked to borrow more books from school. Some of the parents took over the running of the monthly group meetings. In short, they became empowered through learning to interpret literature in relation to their own experience and reality. Returning to the dilemma proposed by Goldenberg *et al* (1992), the parents learned new practices and at the same time built on their existing cultural skills and knowledge.

In a follow-up intervention in the same community as the study (Delgado-Gaitan, 1990) referred to earlier, Delgado-Gaitan (1994) describes a culturally and linguistically appropriate Family Literacy Project, run initially by the researcher and then taken over by the parents. Building on the previous study by Ada (1988), the main focus of analysis for Delgado-

Gaitan was the question-response interaction in the literacy activity in the home. In parent-training meetings the parents worked together to devise questions to ask their children about the particular texts they would bring home. Before the intervention project began, parents and children were recorded reading together. Although parents read to their children in most of the families, the data revealed that all but one set of parents listened to their children read without much verbal interaction. Some parents did not listen to their children read but handed this role to a sibling. The texts for the home reading project were selected so that they were culturally and linguistically familiar to the parents and so that parents would be able to ask questions which developed cultural and critical literacies as well as functional literacy. As parents read more with their children and became more experienced, they developed a more expanded repertoire of questions. Researchers found that parents did not need to be guided to ask questions in the four categories prescribed in the Ada study; they generated questions of their own which fitted the categories well. Parents increased their confidence in dealing with schools because they developed more experience in academic tasks. This was revealed in follow-up interviews a year after the intervention project finished.

Delgado-Gaitan (1994) concluded that through question-and-answer text interactions parents and children shared values and opinions about the importance of the family, identity with a group, emotional support and freedom. Increased awareness among parents was evidenced by a positive change in their self-perception and efficacy in being able to participate directly in their children's literacy learning. Although the project was designed to deal only with family literacy within the home, the effects extended beyond the household. Families became empowered on numerous levels beyond the home reading activity as parents became knowledgeable about the importance of encouraging literacy in the home, learning collectively with other community members and becoming more involved in their children's education through an established parent group. In a further commentary on this project, Delgado-Gaitan (1996) summarised some of the outcomes of the family reading programme: family interactions were enhanced, specifically between parents and children; through increased parent-child communication, parents became more efficacious advocates; schools became more responsive to the Latino community; teacher-parent communication increased by over sixty per cent. Individual parents' self-perception was transformed, as they began to dismiss stereotypes they had previously internalised that characterised them as incompetent and even uncaring parents. This sense of critical reflection and enhanced self-esteem through engagement with literacy interactions which build on cultural and linguistic strengths became a process of empowerment for these minority language families.

Summary

The evidence from research studies conducted in minority communities is that literacy (like 'illiteracy') has different meanings in different societies, in different groups within a society, and between different households in societal groups. For some families literacy as it is constructed by the dominant culture and manifested in schools' demands to read English books at home paves the way to empowerment and academic success, but for others the literacy demanded by the school is intimidating and beyond their reach. Parent education programmes may offer strategies to such families, but these are most effective when they build on existing knowledge and cultural resources. Minority families may feel that in order to achieve even partial success in meeting the demands of the school, they are required to cast off their own cultural identity and adopt aspects of the dominant culture. In any case, parents who do not speak, read or write English may prefer to leave the education of their children to the teachers in the school.

Attempts to involve parents in the education of their children may fail to reach the parents who are most in need of support. Thus parental involvement programmes may increase educational inequality, as precious resources are expended on those who are most accessible to teachers and least need support. However, as Delgado-Gaitan (1990, 1994, 1996) has demonstrated, there is much that can be done by schools to involve all parents in their children's education, despite apparent difficulties of communication and access. In the next chapters the voices of minority-language parents and the teachers of their children articulate the successes and at times frustrations of the home-school learning process, as one school sought to involve parents in the education of young children in an urban setting.

4

BANGLADESHI CHILDREN'S READING AT HOME AND SCHOOL

Introduction

Until recently, research in the field of second language learning and bilingualism had remained largely separate from research which studied literacy and literacies (Ferdman and Weber, 1994). However, both Europe and North America have in the last several years become host to many migrant groups who have brought with them rich and diverse literacies. To understand the linguistic and cultural experiences of these minority groups in Western societies, studies are needed which make clear the process of school-related literacy learning in minority communities. My research sets out to do this by investigating the specific strategies used by minority-language parents as they respond to the task of helping their children to read school books at home. By observing reading sessions at home and at school I could compare the reading support strategies used by teachers and by family members in their respective settings. In interviews with parents and teachers, each group was invited to reflect on the process of Bangladeshi children's English literacy learning and the ways in which families, especially mothers, were empowered or disempowered in their attempts to support this process. A number of questions provided starting-points for the study:

- How do Bangladeshi families respond to the task of supporting their children reading school books at home?

- What are teachers' expectations of Bangladeshi parents as home literacy tutors?

- What are Bangladeshi parents' attitudes to their role as home literacy tutor?

- How do Bangladeshi families' home literacies contribute to their children's school literacy learning?

Methods in studying literacy in a multilingual community

It was in a school with a high minority-language population that my investigation of questions about literacy, power and social justice began. The methodological approaches and techniques I used to investigate the language and literacy interactions between a group of minority-language families and their children's school is now outlined.

The research setting

Before I began the research, I had been a teacher in multilingual primary schools, where I taught many Bangladeshi children, and found that their parents were often the least visible at the school. At the same time, evidence was emerging (Gillborn and Gipps, 1996) that Bangladeshi children were not attaining as highly as other groups in the primary years. Accordingly I chose to investigate questions of literacy, power and social justice in the context of interactions between Bangladeshi families and their children's teachers. The study focused on a single school, 'Valley Community Primary School', in an inner-city area of a large metropolitan conurbation in central England. At the time of data collection, 21 per cent of children in the school were of Bangladeshi origin and 73 per cent of Pakistani origin. The remainder were of a variety of groups, including Malay, White British and African-Caribbean. The school provided a large number of placements for teacher education students who were attached to local and remote institutions of higher education. I had taught at the school for three years so I was known to some of the staff and I already had some knowledge of the local community. The school was highly regarded by the local education authority as a successful school which worked positively with its community and had recently been awarded Community Primary School status.

Having chosen the school, I selected the children. They had to be Bangladeshi, six years old, and in Year Two of their primary schooling, so that they had been in school for more than two years at the time of data collection. Choosing children in their third year of schooling would allow parents and teachers to reflect on the process of the children's literacy learning. Twenty children in the school met these criteria but two of the children's parents would or could not become involved in the research, reducing the number of participating families to eighteen.

All the children were born in Britain to Bangladeshi immigrant parents, ten of them boys and eight girls. Ten of the children's fathers were un-employed at the time and the rest were employed in restaurants, one of them part-time. As the data were collected and analysed, the children's mothers became important participants in the study. All had been born in Bangladesh and migrated to Britain between 1978 and 1987 (Table 1) and most had attended school for five or six years in Bangladesh, although three had never been to school. These families spoke Sylheti at home. All the women reported that their children spoke English to each other and Sylheti to parents and other adults at home. All the women were able to read and write Bengali (the standard language of Bangladesh), except the three who had not attended school (Table 2). None of the eighteen said that she read, wrote or spoke English with confidence.

The role of the bilingual/bicultural research assistant

A bilingual/bicultural research assistant was required to provide inter-pretation and translation skills, to be able to negotiate access to the women participants' homes, and to be culturally compatible with them. My most pressing reason for recruiting a bilingual/bicultural research assistant to help collect data was that I cannot speak Sylheti and the women respondents could not speak English. I approached Mrs Minara Miah, who had been employed by the subject school as a part-time Com-munity Link Worker until shortly before the data collection began and she agreed to support the research project. Mrs Miah is a Bangladeshi woman who speaks Sylheti as a first language and English as an additional language. She has three young children, two of whom attended the subject school but were not involved in my study. Mrs Miah's social network consisted largely of Bangladeshi women whose young children attended the subject school so she was already known to most of the families who became participants in the study.

Part of Mrs Miah's function as research assistant involved acting as cultural broker in initiating the participation of the mothers of the eighteen children. Gaining the parents' agreement to become involved in the research involved far more than interpreting skills. After explaining the aims of the research, Mrs Miah negotiated access to the home and permission to record the child reading a school book at home, and sought agreement that I could interview the parent a week or so later, with herself as interpreter.

Table 1: Background data of the women participants, all born in Bangladesh

Name of child	Education	Stay in UK	No. children	Husband's employment
Lilu	10 years	11 years	six	chef
Shopna	9 years	10 years	five	chef
Belal	6 years	12 years	five	waiter
Taslima	9 years	8 years	six	chef
Mohd. Ali	10 years	10 years	three	chef
Rubina	none	8 years	eight	unemployed
Sultanas	6 years	9 years	five	waiter (p/t)
Dilwar	3 years	9 years	seven	unemployed
Mamun	5 years	15 years	six	waiter
Joyghun	none	11 years	eight	unemployed
Mahbubur	3 years	8 years	six	unemployed
Hussain Ali	6 years	10 years	four	waiter
Aminur	5 years	10 years	eight	unemployed
Husna	none	10 years	six	unemployed
Muhitur	6 years	13 years	four	unemployed
Rahima	5 years	18 years	four	unemployed
Rabia	5 years	8 years	six	unemployed
Naim	14 years	11 years	two	unemployed

Table 2: Individual Bangladeshi mothers' self-reported English and Bengali literacy proficiency

child's name	read Bengali	write Bengali	read English	write English	speak English	comprehend English
Lilu	very good	very good	no	no	no	no
Shopna	very good	very good	no	no	no	no
Belal	very good	very good	not very good	not very good	no	not very good
Taslima	very good	very good	no	no	no	no
Mohd. Ali	not very good	not very good	no	no	no	not very good
Sultanas	very good	very good	no	no	no	not very good
Rubina	no	no	no	no	no	no
Dilwar	very good	very good	not very good	not very good	not very good	not very good
Mamun	very good	very good	not very good	no	no	not very good
Joyghun	no	no	no	no	no	not very good
Mahbubur	very good	very good	no	no	no	not very good
Hussain Ali	not very good	not very good	no	no	no	not very good
Aminur	very good	very good	no	no	no	not very good
Husna	no	no	no	no	no	no
Muhitur	very good	very good	not very good	not very good	no	not very good
Rahima	very good	very good	no	not very good	no	not very good
Rabia	good	very good	no	no	no	not very good
Naim	very good	very good	good	good	not very good	not very good

Data collection

Data were collected in reading sessions at home and at school, and in interviews with the parents and teachers of the eighteen children.

Home literacy observation

With negotiations complete and appointments to visit secured, Mrs Miah, equipped with a dictaphone-type cassette recorder, visited each family. The visits usually took place after school, either immediately before or after the children went to the mosque, for those who attended. The audio-cassette recorder was fitted to the subject children in a small 'bum-bag' belted round the waist and a small 'tie-clip' microphone attached to their outer clothing, at lapel level. Mrs Miah asked the children to read in whatever way they usually did when they read school books a home. In all but one case the child reading was given help by a sibling during the focused observation. In the exceptional case, the child (Naim) was supported by his mother. In some reading sessions children read several texts but most concentrated on a single book. In several cases the child's mother or father directed the reading session by, for example, asking the child to go and get a book. In one reading session between Lilu and his nine-year-old sister, more than six hundred separate utterances were recorded, all referring to the text. Other observations were shorter and included fewer utterances. All eighteen children successfully recorded a reading session, the shortest being eleven minutes and the longest thirty-five. Mrs Miah did not intervene during the observations.

School literacy observation

Within two weeks of the recordings of these home literacy interactions, the children were recorded reading to their teachers in the classroom. The teachers took responsibility for the recordings themselves and used the same audio-cassette recorder as used for the home recordings. They were given the same request to listen to the children read in whatever way was usual and again there was no attempt to collect broader language or literacy data. Fifteen recordings of reading interactions were made, one involving three children reading the same text and another involving two, as one of the teachers was using a 'group reading' technique. The other thirteen reading sessions recorded were all reading interactions between one child and one teacher. Some of the recordings were conducted during school assembly time, or at other periods when the teacher was not engaged with the whole class and this produced good quality recordings for transcription.

Interviews with the Bangladeshi women

Within seven days of recording their children reading at home, the children's mothers were interviewed about their children's literacy learning. My interview questions interpreted in Sylheti by Mrs Miah, gave the women opportunities to talk about their interactions with the school as they tried to support their children's literacy learning, and to talk about broader issues of language and literacy use in the home. When collecting interview data in the homes of Spanish-speaking families in California, Delgado-Gaitan (1990, 1993) found a good deal of apprehension on the part of parents, who would gather their children together in the living room, while only the parents would speak for the family. She asked the families to go about their usual business, but the presence of the researcher altered the usual family routine. Interviews were also problematic as the parents would often give cryptic responses of only a word or two in answer to her interview questions. Although she shared the same language as the respondents in her study, Delgado-Gaitan was evidently still regarded as an outsider: as a highly-educated academic, she was not a member of the group she was interviewing.

The role of Mrs Miah as interpreter in the interviews with Bangladeshi women provided an invaluable bridge between me as outsider researcher and the women as respondents. The interviews always took place in the living-room of the family home. Mrs Miah would usually position herself somewhere between me and the interviewee, although sometimes she sat beside the respondent, so both women faced me – usually when the interviewee seemed apprehensive. Mrs Miah interpreted my questions and the women's responses in manageable sections. This meant that Mrs Miah sometimes interrupted the respondent so that she could interpret what had been said. Mrs Miah was accustomed to the role of interpreter at the school while she was Community Link Worker, so this process ran smoothly.

In designing the interview protocol it was necessary to ask questions which focused on the issues which were the concern of the study, but which also gave the respondents opportunities to raise their own concerns (Powney and Watts, 1987). Each interview began with closed questions about language use and demographic data, which enabled the women to give clear, informative answers to unambiguous questions and so develop confidence as an interview respondent, since they were talking about themselves and no controversy was associated with the questions or answers. Subsequent questions were more open, inviting the women to express their attitudes and concerns about their children's literacy learning. Having gained confidence from answering closed questions, most of the women responded more fully to relatively open questions. When the parents were reticent, prompts such as 'Can you say more about that?' or 'why is that?' were used to encourage a fuller response. All the women agreed to allow the interviews to be audio-cassette recorded, once confidentiality was guaranteed. The schedule was designed so that everyone was asked much the same set of questions and these were supported by prompts which encouraged the women to expand their response. In addition, questions were asked which arose from the informants' answers.

Martin-Jones (1995, 1989) notes that in sociolinguistic surveys, respondents' self-reports of language use may be idealisations of actual communicative practices. I made no attempt to collect the full range of naturalistic speech data in the Bangladeshi households, as language and literacy use *per se* was not the focus of the research questions. Consequently the women's self-reports of their language use could not be formally checked against recorded data. However, Mrs Miah, who knew the Bangladeshi women as part of her social network, corroborated the women's statements about their language use and proficiency.

Interviews with teachers

I interviewed the three class teachers of the eighteen children in the study. The intention was to give them the opportunity to talk about how they supported parents' efforts to teach their children to read. I structured the interviews so that the initial questions allowed the teachers to explain their strategies for teaching reading in the classroom, followed by questions about involving parents in the home. This allowed the teachers to talk freely about teaching children to read, and to develop confidence as interview respondents. As in the interviews with the Bangladeshi women, prompts were used if answers seemed incomplete. In addition, questions which had not been written in the interview schedule were asked in response to the teachers' replies.

Home and school strategies for hearing young Bangladeshi children read

During one of the interviews, a child's mother explained in Sylheti why she had not taken a role herself in the child's reading of a school book at home:

> It's very hard to teach the children at home because I don't speak English. I am trying my very best

All the women interviewed expressed their wish to support their children's school literacy learning and many tried to offer support even though the texts were in a language in which they were not literate:

> I can't put the words together, I can't explain them, but I try to help with the spelling out, I spell the words

Seventeen of the eighteen women asked their other children (some as young as eight) to help the six-year-old to read a school book.

To analyse the reading sessions, I used a system of ten categories, adapted from the Hannon *et al* (1986) study referred to in Chapter Two and developed from the recordings of the Bangladeshi children reading with support at home and at school. As in Hannon *et al*'s system of analysis, a 'move' was an intervention in the reading process made by the sibling or adults involved.

1. *Emphasising meaning.* Moves were coded in this category if they reflected the teacher's or home reading aide's concern that the child had understood the text. These moves were usually questions about the meaning of words or phrases, or questions about their under-standing of the story. For example, Mahbubur's teacher asked him:

   > why couldn't Mum get the breakfast, what was she going to be doing?

2. *Providing a reading model*. Data were coded in this category if the teacher or home reading aide read a section of the text to the child. For example, Rahima's sister demonstrated how to read with appropriate expression:

> you have to put some impression in: I wonder what this is she said, my mum had to say sorry

3. *Insisting on accuracy.* Moves were coded in this category if they insisted that the text be read accurately, when a semantically acceptable substitution for the correct word had been offered. Such substitutions included corrections to miscues such as 'a' for 'the', as in the following example from Muhitur's home reading session with his sister, as he reads *The Emperor's New Clothes*:

> M: a wardrobe master entered the throne room
> MS: the wardrobe master
> M: that's what I said
> MS: you said a wardrobe master you should say the wardrobe master

If the child's error did affect the sense, the move which followed the miscue was coded according to which features of text were addressed, for example the meaning of the sentence (*Category 5*), or the parts of the word (*Category 4*).

4. *Decoding* Moves were placed in this category if they referred to children's phonic knowledge, for example sound-symbol correspondence. An example of data coded in this category is the following, as Dilwar's teacher supports his reading:

> T: what sounds can you see in that word?
> D: ea
> T: ea
> D: sy
> T: put it all together
> D: ea (..) sy
> T: easy
> D: easy

In this interaction three teacher moves required the child to use his phonic knowledge.

5. *Using understanding*. Moves were coded in this category if they encouraged the child to draw on knowledge of the textual context or of semantics. In the following example, Lilu is reading to his teacher:

L: there's a tiny light to stop you began scared Little Bear

T: wait a minute wait a minute does that make sense? There's a tiny light to stop you began scared

In this move the teacher repeated the miscue, and gave Lilu the opportunity to use his semantic knowledge to self-correct.

6. *Providing words and phrases*. Moves were coded in this category if the teacher or home reading aide provided the next word or phrase in the text. This move could be made immediately following the previous word, or after a pause or miscue. In the following example, Joyghun is reading to her sister:

J: whatever have you got there it's not a (...) what (..) said(..)
JS: Jody
J: Jody it's a bear his name is Paddlington
JS: Paddington
J: and he's coming to stay with us (3)
JS: mercy me
J: mercy me cried Mrs Bird

In this example Joyghun's sister provides words and phrases to correct Joyghun's miscue ('Paddlington'), and to give Joyghun access to unfamiliar words ('Jody', and 'mercy').

7. *Praise*. Moves were coded in this category when children were praised for their reading. For example, in the following example Rabia's teacher praised her efforts in reading unfamiliar words:

R: called (..) I'm coming
T: good girl
R: but as she climbed on to the roof the ladder came tumbling
T: good girl you say it then

R: tumbling
T: good girl
R: down
T: good girl it came tumbling down didn't it

8. *Criticism*. Moves were coded in this category if they were general criticisms which did not refer to specific reading strategies. For example, Lilu's sister expressed her criticism of Lilu as follows:

LS: you should know the words, you're a silly boy doesn't
      learn anything

More specific criticisms which referred to specific errors in reading were coded according to the kind of response made, for example criticism might be associated with an instruction to look at the initial sound of the word (*Category 4*), or to take account of the meaning of the sentence (*Category 5*).

9. *Directions* Moves were coded in this category if they were concerned with the management and organisation of the reading session, rather than the reading itself. In the following example, Muhitur's mother intervenes in Sylheti, after he has finished reading a book to his sister:

MM: come here go and read something else
M: I haven't got anything else to read
MM: go and read a Bengali book

10. *Unrelated talk.* Data were coded in this category when talk was un-related to the reading session. For example, the following interaction was recorded between Naim and his mother:

N: Mum (..) tv (..) I want to watch tv
NM: you want to watch tv?

All of the moves made by teachers and home reading aides were coded.

Reading at home and at school

The families' attempts to support their six-year-old's English literacy, using a text brought home from school by the child, constituted the school-focused home literacy interactions. Eighteen home literacy interactions were recorded. In all, 1604 moves were identified in the eighteen home reading interactions and 673 in the school reading interactions. The codes and the number and percentage of moves in each category, are presented in Table 3. Home reading aides (seventeen of the eighteen were siblings, some as young as eight) used one move considerably more frequently than any other: more than eighty per cent of moves were to provide the next word or phrase in the text. In comparison, only six per cent of the moves made by teachers came into this category. The difference between the extent to which teachers and home reading aides provided the next word or phrase in the text revealed the major difference between reading support strategies at school and home. By providing the next word or phrase, often before the reader had tried to read it, the sibling was not teaching the six-year-old to use independent reading strategies,

Table 3: Number of moves in each category by home reading aides and teachers expressed as an aggregate and percentage of their moves

Category of move	School: agg.	Home: agg.	School (%)	Home (%)
1. Emphasising meaning	284	29	42.2	1.81
2. Providing a reading model	10	13	1.49	0.81
3. Insisting on accurancy	1	21	0.15	1.31
4. Decoding	79	22	11.74	1.37
5. Using understanding	125	31	18.57	1.93
6. Providing words and phrases	41	1289	6.09	80.36
7. Praise	86	13	12.78	0.81
8. Criticism	0	4	0	0.25
9. Directions	47	150	6.98	9.35
10. Unrelated talk	0	32	0	2
All moves	673	1604	100	100

Table 4: Moves made in response to children's miscues and hesitations expressed as an aggregate and percentage of their moves in response to miscues and hesitations

Category of move	School: agg.	Home: agg.	School (%)	Home (%)
3. Insisting on accuracy	1	21	0.41	1.54
4. Decoding	79	22	32.11	1.61
5. Using understanding	125	31	50.81	2.27
6. Providing words and phrases	41	1289	16.66	94.57
All moves which were responses to miscues and hesitations	246	1363	100	100

but was relying on a narrow range of moves to support the child's school-related reading.

Other differences between the teachers' reading support strategy and that used in home reading interactions referred to the extent to which the meaning of the text was emphasised. Over 42 per cent of moves made by teachers were questions or explanations concerned to establish that the child had understood the text. In contrast, only 1.8 per cent of moves made in home reading interactions were concerned that the subject child had understood the text. It is again clear that the strategies used by families for teaching children to read were very different from those used by the teachers. There was also a clear difference between the strategies used at home and at school when a child made a miscue or hesitated over an unfamiliar word. Analysed as a proportion of their moves in response to miscues and hesitations, the teachers asked children to attend to the meaning of the text on 50.8 per cent of occasions (Table 4). Home reading aides, however, used this kind of move on just 2.3 per cent of the 1363 occasions that they responded to the subject child's miscues or hesitations.Whereas 15 per cent of moves made in home reading interactions were not in response to miscues or hesitations, this was true of 63.4 per cent of moves made in school reading sessions. This suggests that teachers were more prepared to take the initiative in a reading session and talk about the text, whereas home reading aides passively waited for errors or hesitations to occur. There were obvious differences between the school reading support strategy and the home reading support strategy.

Bangladeshi children reading school books at home

A closer analysis of the reading interaction data reveals that the strategies used by siblings to support their younger brothers' and sisters' reading were markedly similar across the group. Putting aside the one home literacy interaction which involved a parent, the other seventeen reading sessions were characterised by a very narrow range of moves by the reading aides, who relied very largely on providing the next word in the text when the reader hesitated or got it wrong. Rahima's ten-year-old sister demonstrated a reading support strategy which relied on her reading each word, and six-year-old Rahima repeating it, as they read a version of *The King of Spain's Daughter*:

R   nothing
RS   would
R   would it
RS   bear
R   bear
RS   but
R   but a
RS   silver
R   silver
RS   nutmeg
R   nutmeg and a
RS   golden
R   golden
RS   pear
R   pear

Rahima's sister intervened in this reading session 130 times, of which 100 moves were to provide the next word or phrase in the text. But it was clear that Rahima could read more fluently than she was allowed in most of the interaction with her sister. When she had an opportunity, she read:

opened the door to see that the King of Spain's daughter...

Also, during her recorded reading session with her teacher, Rahima read fluently as follows:

'I'm scared' said Little Bear, 'Why are you scared, Little Bear?' asked Big Bear. 'I don't like the dark', said Little Bear. 'What dark?' asked Big Bear. 'The dark ... the dark all around us', said Little Bear. 'But I brought you a lantern', said Big Bear

These data suggest that in her determination to help, Rahima's ten-year-old sister was restricting her reading opportunities. A more dramatic picture emerged in the interaction between Lilu and his nine-year-old sister. Of 309 moves made by the nine-year-old in a lengthy reading session, 307 were to give the next word or phrase (the other two moves were coded as *Criticism*). Much of the session was a reading of *The Lord's Prayer*. Typically, the children read as follows:

LS hallowed
L   hallowed
LS be thy
L   be thy
LS name
L   name

Once again, when he had an opportunity, Lilu demonstrated that he was capable of doing more than repeat his sister's reading of individual words and phrases, as he read without hesitation:

praise for happy days, thank you for each happy day, for fun

Just as in Rahima's case, Lilu demonstrated in his classroom reading session with his teacher that he could read without needing support with every word:

Big Bear put Little Bear in the dark part of the cave (..) 'Go to sleep Little Bear', he said, and Little Bear tried

Like Rahima's sister, Lilu's nine-year-old sister seemed to prevent him from reading meaningfully, in her enthusiasm to teach her brother.

A similar picture emerged in the interventions made during Taslima's reading to her eight-year-old sister (160 moves in a total of 171 were to provide the next word or phrase), in Mahbubur's reading to his twelve-year-old brother (128 moves in a total of 145 were to provide the next word or phrase), and in Rubina's reading to her eleven-year-old sister (125 moves in a total of 145 were to provide the next word or phrase). However, this strategy was not confined to younger reading aides. Husna's fifteen-year-old brother made 117 moves when listening to his younger sister read, of which all but one were to provide the next word or phrase in the text, and Aminur's fourteen-year-old sister used a similar strategy, with 117 of 123 moves to provide the next word or phrase in the text. Overall, more than eighty per cent of all moves made by home reading aides were to provide the next word or phrase in the text. This strategy did not attend closely to the meaning of what was read, as there was little talk about the text or its content. The sibling reading aides' attempts to support the English literacy learning of the younger children could not be said to be socially meaningful to the young readers (Cummins, 1994a; 1996; Trueba, 1989; Reder, 1994). The interactions were characterised by repetition of given words and scant attention to meaning. There was little sense of collaborative interaction or inquiry.

The one interaction in which a sibling used strategies to check the younger child's understanding of the text served to emphasise the lack of such moves in the others. Muhitur's twelve-year-old sister asked ten questions to check whether he had understood the story of *The Emperor's New Clothes*, which he had just read aloud. However, his responses were not positively received by his twelve-year-old tutor, as in the following example, in which his correct answer is not accepted:

MS were Rick and Rack making invisible clothes or normal clothes?
M   he wasn't making any clothes at all
MS were they invisible?
M   no (...) they were weren't they?
MS yea
M   they were?

Muhitur's sister clearly had some understanding that it was appropriate to ask questions of her brother about his comprehension of the text but this particular interaction may have confused Muhitur rather than consolidating what was apparently a good understanding of the story. Notwithstanding the flaw in this attempt to attend to the meaning of the story, it is an exceptional case among the sibling reading support data, as no other siblings ever asked questions about the meaning of the text. This interaction emphasises that the sibling reading aides generally used a narrow range of moves, which did not attend to the meaning of the text. This is not to say that the siblings' efforts were unhelpful or necessarily less effective than the teachers' interventions but their strategy was certainly quite different.

The data present a clear picture of families mobilising whatever resources were available in their efforts to support their children's English literacy learning. However, the families were disempowered by the siblings' apparent lack of knowledge about the school's reading strategy. This evidence is compared with the parents' responses to questions about school-related reading interactions in the home, and with teachers' practices to support children's reading in the classroom.

Parental aspirations and the literacy process

It is clear from the data presented above that the mothers of these six-year-old Bangladeshi children were sufficiently committed to their sons' and daughters' academic success to call on every available resource in supporting their English literacy learning. But it is equally clear that the women lacked the linguistic skills to enable them to become actively involved in their children's reading of school books at home. This was the cause of some frustration for the parents, as they wanted their children to succeed in the English school system. This frustration was articulated by Aminur's mother:

> I would really like to help Aminur with school reading books, but I don't even speak English, so it's very difficult for me

Some of the parents' interview responses referred explicitly to their commitment to their children's academic success. All the parents considered that it was important for their children to learn English. Shopna's mother's response was typical of the group as a whole: 'if she doesn't learn English she won't do well in school'. Aminur's mother concurred, saying 'English is more important when they are in this country, because they have to study'. Mohammed Ali's mother added a description of her encouragement for her children to learn to read and write English at home:

we have Sky TV but I switch it off because the children should be reading and writing as much as possible. The children have pens and paper in their hands all the time, they are always writing and scribbling, I buy felt pens and paper every week, I have to buy it three times because there are three of them

Mohammed Ali's mother went on to say that she planned to join an English class, because she wanted to give her children more help with their English literacy learning. Other parents indicated their commitment to their children's academic learning in different ways. Mamun's mother said her son...

was not well treated at school at first, he didn't do well with his reading, but he is all right now, he has improved

Mahbubur's mother spoke of her son's enthusiasm for school, saying 'he wants to go to school all the time, even if he has a temperature he wants to go to school'. Sultanas' mother was sufficiently concerned about her children's progress at school to say 'I am looking for a private tutor for my son because he is going downhill'. One of Rabia's sisters had recently begun secondary school and was working so diligently at her homework that she was causing concern to her family:

she's stuck into her studying upstairs, she won't eat until the homework is completed, she overdoes it, and sometimes she gets stressed... we think she should take a break among the two or three hours she does it, she can get herself really worried about her studying

Naim's mother, unusually well-educated with her college education in Bangladesh, said that Naim had to learn English, because all her family was educated, and that was important to her. She said that she was 'encouraging him to read better to make something of himself'. The teachers articulated their understanding of the parents' attitudes to their children's school learning, saying, for example,

I would say definitely they do have a positive attitude to all of the learning, not just the reading, they really want the children to do well

These responses present a picture of parents with considerable commitment to their children's English literacy learning. They were clear about the importance of English literacy to their children's academic success in the school system. But the confidence of the Bangladeshi mothers to support their children's English literacy learning at home was very different from their aspirations for their children.

Parents' role in school-focused reading at home

A majority of the parents said that they could not offer any help to their young children in school-focused home literacy activities. The response from Sultana's mother was typical: 'I can't do it because I can't read English'. The mothers' determination to help their young children to learn was evident, however, in the responses of those who attempted to provide support despite their limited English proficiency, such as the mother of Belal, 'I spell out the words, but I can't make a sentence', and Taslima's mother:

> I can't put the words together, I can't explain them, but I try to help with the spelling out, I spell the words

Naim's mother used a similar strategy:

> I spell it out and read it to him, if the word is very hard I look at the dictionary, the Bengali dictionary, I always carry the dictionary, English to Bengali to English

Implicit in all of these responses is a frustration on the part of the mothers that they were unable to give more support to their children's English literacy learning. The support they could offer was diverse, though, and reached beyond the one-to-one reading interaction in English. Mohammed Ali's mother, for example, made a point of encouraging her children to read: 'the children have six or seven books, I tell them to read them before they go to bed', while Hussain Ali's mother made a deliberate attempt to provide resources for literacy learning: 'I give them pens and paper and they write and draw, that sort of thing'. The parents' commitment to their children's English literacy learning is visible in these responses. Their determination to support their children's learning, despite their feelings of helplessness to accomplish this effectively, was consistent with the findings of a range of studies in minority-language communities (Delgado-Gaitan, 1990; Chavkin and Williams, 1993; Vincent, 1996; Simich-Dudgeon, 1993). Each of these studies found that families which had difficulties in providing active support for their children's education were nevertheless very committed to their children's school-focused learning.

Two of the parents spoke of using home language strategies to support their children's English literacy learning. Naim's mother – the only parent centrally involved in any of the recorded literacy interactions in the home – described a home literacy session with her son which had been recorded a few days earlier. Naim had read the story of *Jack and the Beanstalk* in English, and his mother asked him a range of questions in Sylheti to check that he had understood what he had read:

NM what have you read?
N   first (..) the boy had a beanstalk
NM no
N   first he went outside with the cow
NM who did he go with?
N   the cow (...) he went to market
NM what was he going to do with the cow?
N   he went to sell the cow
NM to sell (..) then what happened? say what happened then

Of the 31 moves in this reading interaction, 18 were concerned to check that Naim had understood the text and was able to relate the story. When interviewed, Naim's mother had a clear rationale for her strategy in supporting her child's reading:

I wanted to know, I asked Naim to tell it in our language to find out if it is really going into his head or is he just reading it, I wanted to know, and I can't read it, well I can read it, but I want to know what is really happening, is it going in there or is he just reading

In this instance Naim's mother used the resources available to her – her own language – to check that her son had understood the text of the school reading book. Her English literacy was not confident but she found a way of supporting her son's school-related reading. These examples again presented a vivid picture of parents who had considerable commitment to their children's academic learning and were prepared to make use of whatever resources they could find. The Bangladeshi parents were greatly

committed to their children's academic learning but they felt frustrated by
their lack of skills or knowledge to support it effectively.

Bangladeshi children reading at school

The teachers' strategy for teaching reading was apparent in the reading
sessions recorded in the school. In contrast to the sibling reading aides,
they used a broad range of moves in classroom reading interactions and
refrained almost entirely from providing children with the next word or
phrase in the text. The teachers emphasised the meaning of the text more
than any other move. In the following example, Lilu is reading to his
teacher:

L: there's a tiny light to stop you began scared Little Bear

T: wait a minute wait a minute does that make sense? There's a tiny
   light to stop you began scared

In this move the teacher repeated the miscue, allowing Lilu to use his
semantic knowledge to self-correct. In most of the classroom literacy
interactions teachers were teaching the children to focus on the meaning
of the text and talk about the text, rather than simply have them read the
words without discussion. The teachers' interventions were characterised
by questions such as:

stop there for a minute, what do you think is going to happen next?

In another example, a teacher discusses with Sultanas a story about a
child's first day at school:

it's hard when you first try tying your laces isn't it? When you were
little could you tie yours? It was hard when you first tried though
wasn't it? Did you think it was? It is, because your fingers won't do
what you want them to will they?

Here the teacher sought to extend Sultanas' understanding beyond the
world of text, so that the reading interaction was meaningful to the child.
The balance of moves used by the teachers indicated that teachers' reading support strategies were far more concerned with the meaning of the
text than were the interventions at home. The teachers' practice in teaching reading was consistent with their belief, expressed at follow-up inter-

views, that children should be taught a range of independent reading skills.

In the following example, Dilwar is reading the story of *Peter and the Wolf* to his teacher. The teacher asks Dilwar to deduce meanings from the text, and praises him when he introduces new vocabulary:

D: Out came Peter's grandfather, 'Come here Peter', he said, 'You must come home with me, it's not safe out here in the meadow, a wolf may come and get you'.

T: Why does grandfather think it's dangerous?

D: Because the wolf will get Peter

T: Yes wolves are dangerous creatures aren't they?

D: Yea they're wild

T: they're wild that's right good boy

When a child hesitated at an unfamiliar word or made an error, the teachers usually offered contextual support and asked the child to try again, rather than simply giving the correct reading of the word. Teachers regularly made explicit to children the independent reading strategies they were teaching them to use, including self-correction, re-reading sentences and using picture cues.

Discussion

The school-focused reading interaction data collected in the homes and classrooms of these Bangladeshi children clearly demonstrate that the children were being supported by teachers and siblings in very different ways. In seventeen of the home recordings, siblings were supporting the young children using a narrow range of interventions, whereas the classroom recordings revealed that teachers used a strategy which incorporated a broader range of moves. The preponderance of the siblings' 'copy-and-repetition' interventions may be explained in terms of their assumptions about how best to teach reading. This interpretation is consistent with Goldenberg *et al*'s (1992) study, which found that Hispanic families engaged in school-focused literacy activities by correcting the child for each word read not as written. We saw in Chapter Three how Goldenberg *et al* proposed that this practice showed the families' views and assumptions about how to teach children to read. It may be that the siblings of the young Bangladeshi children at Valley Community Primary School were drawing on reading interaction patterns encountered at mosque and/or community school which most of them attended. So their reading support strategy may have derived, at least in part, from the model of copy-and-repetition prevalent in these settings (Gregory, 1996a; 1996b).

However, such an analysis is incomplete if it disregards the broader interactions of power between school and family. The children's mothers made it clear that they felt largely unsupported by the school in their efforts to help their children to read the books they brought home from school. School books were sent home with young children without any explicit advice or instructions about how best to use them. The school books were in English, which was not the language of literacy for these parents so parents felt frustrated and 'disempowered' (Gregory, 1996b) because they wanted to support their children's English literacy learning but were unable to do so. For this reason they made the best of their family resources and involved older siblings in the school-focused literacy support process. The siblings' reading support strategy may have been less to do with their ideas about how to teach reading than with making the best of a difficult task.

What schools can do

What can schools do to ensure that the process of children reading school books at home runs more smoothly? We have seen that reports of best practice indicate that the divide between home and school is reduced when culturally appropriate texts are used, when teachers have a good knowledge of the home literacy environments of the children's families, and when parents have a definite understanding of what the school expects of them as literacy tutors.

The choice of resources for children to read at home with their families is crucial. In my study of the literacy practices of Bangladeshi families, the parents said that most of the children took reading books home from school on a regular basis, with a new book chosen at least once a week and as often as every day. The teachers' interview responses reveal, however, that the school was not entirely committed to the school-focused home reading process in resource terms. The books taken home were not of the same quality as the reading books selected for school use:

> the books that the children take home are not necessarily appropriate to them, they make their own choices about what they read; and also again over the year they're getting wear and tear so they're not as good quality as the kind of ones that we use as reading material.

There are two points here: the books for reading at home were not of the same 'quality' as those used at school; and children often chose books which were inappropriate to their reading level. There was evidence in the home reading sessions that some of the books taken home by the children were indeed inappropriate to their reading levels. An example of this is the following interaction between Mahbubur and his twelve-year-old brother:

M   I know that's too hard for me (..) I can't read that (..) down the rabbit hole (2) I don't know what does that say alice ali was was trying

MB tired

M   tired of (3) s (..) sh (..)

MB spell it out

M   I don't know it's too hard

Only one of the children in the present study was a member of the public library, and most of the children had no or very few English books of their own. The books used for English literacy learning in the home, then, were mainly the books taken home from school, which according to the teachers were of inferior quality, and which may have been at inappropriate levels for the children. As one of the teachers said, 'if you feel that you're going to lose books or get books damaged they don't go home'. This policy, while understandable on economic grounds, may have impeded the home reading process, as the books taken home seemed to be difficult for the children to read and may have been less attractive and interesting than books the children read at school. As school budgets are stretched, it may be difficult for Head Teachers and subject leaders to spend increasing amounts of money on books which are at risk of damage or loss when taken home by children. However, to fail to resource children's reading at home properly may be a false economy, as those children whose families are least able to afford to buy new books may be disadvantaged by having access only to inappropriate texts. A number of schools have taught children to respect and care for books from the very earliest stage of schooling, providing strong, plastic carriers marked with the school logo, and asking parents to take responsibility for the care of the books. Many schools report that in these cases school books generally come back to school in good condition.

A second issue in the resourcing of minority-language children's reading of school books at home is that of *dual language* books. A policy of resourcing children's home reading through books in which the text is in more than one language implies, firstly, that the teachers know which is the appropriate literate language for each family; and secondly, that the children's parents are literate in any language. There may be a hundred or more spoken and written languages among the families of a multilingual school. The use of dual-text books depends on the teachers' knowledge of which families are literate in which languages. It is therefore important that schools are as thorough as possible about gaining accurate information concerning the literacies of the families. This can be done in a number of ways, including home visits by bilingual school staff, classroom workshops for parents, after-school meetings and invitations to parents to choose dual-language books from a range provided. The specific strategy will be determined by the needs of the local community. The question of whether parents are literate in any language should be handled sensitively by school staff, as many parents may be embarrassed about being unable to read or write. The best dual-text books are often written from the perspective of the home culture and translated into English, rather than vice-versa, making them more culturally relevant than books written from an Anglo-centric perspective and translated into the community language.

We should not assume that minority-language parents (or, as we have seen here, siblings) know what to do with the book their young child brings home from school. There is a good deal of evidence (Toomey, 1993) that parents are more effective supporters of their children's reading of school books when they have a clear and confident understanding of what the school expects of them. In my study, the Bangladeshi parents said that they had been told little or nothing about how to support their children's reading. Some had been told to 'make up a story from the pictures'. All said that they would like more information about how to help their children to learn to read their school books.

However, much can be done to develop parents' confidence in supporting their children's reading, even when the parents cannot read English. The Delgado-Gaitan (1996, 1994, 1990; Delgado-Gaitan and Trueba, 1991) study referred to in Chapter Three demonstrates that by listening to the concerns of minority parents and designing a literacy support framework based on their needs, schools can make a considerable difference to parents' confidence in teaching their children to read. In some communities this will mean developing a Family Literacy Project, with appropriate interpreters and resources. This may be based in a local community centre or library, if the school proves to be an intimidating environment for some parents. In other schools it will mean regular home visits to those parents who are unable or unwilling to come to the school.

In the Delgado-Gaitan study, parents became supporters of each other, as certain parents took a lead and helped others to become confident readers with their children. Many of the parents became more active in their involvement with the school in ways which transcended simply reading with their children. This success owed much to the school listening to the minority-language parents' perceptions of the difficulties they encountered in meeting the teachers' expectations, and acting on this information in ways which were consistent with the parents' needs. As David Corson (1994) points out, 'only a local community can really decide what is necessary'. As much of classroom practice is increasingly prescribed from the centre, it is crucial that home-school reading policy is more responsive than ever to the needs of parents at the local level.

Summary

This chapter outlines the methodological tools and techniques used in investigating the process of school-related literacy-learning in a Bangladeshi community in Britain. It presents data which provided a close-up of young Bangladeshi children reading school books at home and at school, with the support of family members and teachers. There were clear differences between the reading support strategies adopted by the school teachers and the young children's siblings, as the siblings adopted a narrow range of types of intervention, possibly based on their notion of how to teach reading or simply their doing their best at literacy instruction when they had little understanding of what the school expected or required of them as literacy tutors. The siblings' efforts were as much a product of their lack of confidence, and lack of knowledge of a range of reading support strategies, as of any clearly defined theory of how to teach reading. The children's parents expressed their frustration that they could not become more directly involved in their young children's school-related reading, suggesting a picture of disempowerment, as the reading task required them to be literate in a language to which they did not have access. In Chapter Five the Bangladeshi women and their children's teachers further define the picture of home-school relations in the reading process.

5
INVOLVING MINORITY-LANGUAGE PARENTS AT SCHOOL

Introduction

While it is widely acknowledged that involvement of parents in the education of their children benefits children's learning, not all parents are equally able to become involved. Some parents have suffered difficult experiences of schooling themselves, leaving them feeling alienated from the formal education process. Others feel less than confident that their views will be valued by professional educators. For minority-language parents, these difficulties are often compounded by speaking a language which is not the language of the school and the problem of not having appropriate interpreters available whenever they want to speak to teachers. These parents may be confident in the domain of their home and community but appear to lack confidence in the majority-culture school. This chapter presents the voices of the Bangladeshi women as they reflected on their attempts to find out information about their children's progress and to communicate with the teachers at Valley Community Primary School, and the voices of the teachers as they articulate their strategy for providing opportunities to communicate with the children's parents. The chapter then considers what schools can do to become effective communicators with parents who seem to be beyond the reach of professionals.

Communicating with Bangladeshi families

The school's strategy for communicating with Bangladeshi families about their children's learning was evident in the parents' and teachers' interview responses which referred to parents' evenings, parents' workshops, a

Bangladeshi women's group, and other informal contacts between teachers and parents.

Parents' evenings

All the women interviewed were asked about their attendance at parents' evenings, which were held two or three times each year with the intention of informing parents about their children's academic progress. The group was equally split between those who said that they went to parents' evenings and those who said they did not. Of the nine mothers who said that they did not attend parents' evenings, five said that their husbands went and one that an older child attended. Of the other three, Lilu's mother said her husband did not go because he was working and that 'Lilu's grandfather used to go, but he is in Bangladesh now'. Similarly, Shopna's mother said 'my husband used to go, but he is working'. The fathers of both Lilu and Shopna were employed as chefs in restaurants, so regularly worked evenings. Among the eighteen families, eight of the children's fathers were employed as chefs or waiters in restaurants – the only source of employment for any of the men. In the third family in which neither of the child's parents attended parents' evening, a different reason was given: Husna's mother said, 'if I go there I won't really understand what's going on, and I'm embarrassed to ask anyone'. Husna's mother obviously felt disempowered in the school context. She did not have confidence that she would understand the teachers. She added,

> I don't know whether they have interpreters, my husband used to take Husna to school but recently he hasn't been very well, so I've been going, but I don't know about interpreters

Husna's mother did not have the crucial information which may have given her access to an understanding of her child's academic progress: she did not know whether a Sylheti interpreter was available at parents' evenings to enable her to speak to the teachers. Either the information about Husna's progress would be given in English, which her mother could not understand, or it would be given in Sylheti through an interpreter. Since Husna's mother did not feel confident enough to find out whether an interpreter was available, she did not attend.

Of the five women who said that only their husbands attended, Taslima's mother reported that although her husband could not understand English sufficiently well to know what the teachers were saying,

> they translate through the children, and the children explain it to my husband, and when they bring the report home Taslima's brother explains the results

Muhitur's mother said, 'my husband goes, I only went when the little one was at nursery, otherwise my husband goes'. Aminur's mother said 'I used to go, but not now, my husband goes now'. The mothers of Mahbubur and Dilwar simply said that their husbands attended parents' evenings. Rubina's mother said 'my older son goes'. In these data is an implication that the women were excluded from first-hand information about their children's academic progress by school structures which did not facilitate their participation in parents' evenings. Possibly these families saw it as the father's role to attend these events but the fact that nine of the mothers *did* regularly attend parents' evenings questions such an assumption. It may have been that the nine women who did not attend simply felt that they lacked the English proficiency required to converse with the teachers. What is clear from these responses is that half the women interviewed did not participate directly at parents' evenings, which the school provided to inform parents about their children's progress.

Of the nine women who said they attended, seven said that they could only understand what the teachers were saying about their children's progress through the interpretation of a family member or friend. Mohammed Ali's mother said that her husband interpreted as best he could:

> He can understand some English, he can't speak much, but he can understand a little, he can get by with it, I don't understand as much

Rabia's mother expressed the same concern as Husna's mother about the question of interpreters:

> We weren't told whether they were providing interpreters, my husband just says 'I can't speak English, it's no use my going'

In both of these examples it seems unlikely that the parents would have felt sufficiently empowered to ask questions of the teachers. Even if they understood some of what the teachers said about their children's progress, their English proficiency would have impeded access to additional information. The parents' responses suggested that the school expected them to learn and use English if they wanted to gain full access to information about their children's schooling.

The remaining five mothers who said that they attended parents' evenings could not understand the teachers easily but asked their children to interpret for them. Sultanas' mother said

> I do understand what the teacher is saying about Sultanas, but I can't speak out so I have Beauty, my daughter, to help me

At the time of the interview Beauty was eight years old. The mothers of both Belal and Mamun took their twelve-year-old sons with them to interpret at parents' evenings. Joyghun's mother said 'I take one of the older children to translate'. Hussain Ali's mother said 'The children tell me what the teacher is saying', which implied that the children who were the subject of the meeting between parent and teacher were also the interpreters. In each of these five cases relatively young children were responsible for communicating the teacher's messages to the parents and perhaps for asking questions of the teachers. Other studies (Vincent, 1996; Sneddon, 1997) of teachers' attempts to communicate with Bangladeshi parents in Britain have found that the only interpreters available in parent-teacher meetings were their own children. Just as the parents were forced to employ their young children as reading aides in the home, so they employed the same children as interpreters when visiting the school. One of the teachers was aware of the difficulty in providing adequate interpreting services at parents' evenings: 'At parents' evenings it's not always easy to talk to the parents because you need an interpreter for each parent'. The parent interview responses suggested that they were unsure about the availability of interpreters at parents' evenings. In reality, provision of adult interpreters was sporadic – there were one or two Bangladeshi interpreters for parents of children visiting fourteen classes during the same evening. The interpreters were untrained and unpaid. It is likely that this situation prevented the parents from asking the teachers questions about any issues concerning their children's education which they preferred not to discuss in front of them.

Parents' workshops

A second context in which the school tried to communicate with the children's parents was through 'parents' workshops', which had been operating in the school until shortly before my interviews began. Parents' workshops were opportunities for parents to spend time in their child's classroom for half an hour at the beginning of the school day, once a week, to find out about and participate in an aspect of the school curriculum. Of the eighteen parents, nine said they had attended a parents' workshop at some time. These parents were generally positive about the opportunity to find out how their children learned in school. Belal's mother said, 'I thought it was good the way they were teaching the children, I liked that, I understand all about it now'. Mohammed Ali's mother was similarly enthusiastic about attending the parents' workshops:

> What happens at the workshop is they just show us how the children are writing, and how they are making things, I do go and sit with them. I watch how they read and write, and I watch how they make things at school

The other seven mothers spoke positively about the workshop and some said that they had taken ideas from it and tried to implement them at home. Sultanas' mother's response was typical: 'What happens at school, I do try and help with at home'. Some of the nine mothers who said they had attended the parents' workshops had not been for some time. Aminur's mother had been ill, so had not attended for two years, while Muhitur's mother could no longer attend 'because of the baby'.

The teachers too were generally positive about the parents' workshops, although their remarks also expressed some reservations. A notable difference between what teachers said about the parents' evenings, and what they said about the parents' workshops, was their reference to the provision of interpreters for the workshops. One of the teachers believed that the parents' workshops had contributed to parents' ability to teach their children to read:

> I think it's helped them to understand how children learn, not just learn to read but how we do things in school. That it is totally different from when we were at school.

On the whole, then, the parents and teachers who had been involved in the parents' workshops were positive about this opportunity for parents to find out about the way their children learned in school. Evidence from other studies (Becker and Epstein, 1982; Dauber and Epstein, 1993) has demonstrated that many minority-culture parents are willing to respond to schools' attempts to involve them in their children's learning, and that teacher practices to involve these parents can make a positive difference to children's literacy attainment. My study of Bangladeshi parents at Valley Community Primary School indicates that the school was at least partially successful in its efforts to make provision for parents to understand the school's processes, and to bridge the divide between minority-language home and dominant-language school.

However, this positive evidence raises questions about why half of the eighteen mothers had never attended the parents' workshops. When comparing the nine mothers who did not attend parents' workshops with those who did not attend parents' evenings, considerable correspondence was found between the two groups, as six of the women appeared in both lists. The mothers of Lilu, Shopna, Taslima, Dilwar, Mahbubur and Husna attended neither parents' evenings nor parents' workshops. Of these, the mothers of Lilu, Shopna and Mahbubur said that they didn't attend the parents' workshops because they had small children to look after at home. Mahbubur's mother said, 'I have to come home because of the babies. Their father is in the house as well, so I can't manage it, because he's off work and the babies are there'. This response is consistent with other research (Karran, 1997), which has found that Bangladeshi women in Britain are sometimes not involved at school because they have work to do at home. Neither Taslima's mother nor Dilwar's gave a reason for their non-attendance at parents' workshops. Husna's mother said 'the teacher asked me to go but I couldn't make it'. When asked why, she replied:

> because you know I can't read or write or understand English, it's a bit embarrassing, I know there's a girl there who will translate, but I feel a bit embarrassed to go. It doesn't look right, the girl is young

Thus Husna's mother recognised that her cultural and linguistic resources would not carry her confidently through the school-based experience, even though she knew there would be an interpreter. She seemed to feel intimidated by the context of the school and referred to the school's predominantly English linguistic environment to describe her 'embarrassment'. In saying that the interpreter was 'young', and that it 'doesn't look right', Husna's mother seemed to imply that a married woman should not talk to teachers through an interpreter who had not yet acquired the same social standing in the community because she was young and unmarried. The interpreter provided by the school was linguistically appropriate for Husna's mother but culturally inappropriate. Despite their attempts to provide the appropriate resources for parents to speak and listen to teachers at parents' workshops, the school had not been able to reach all of the parents. Six of the eighteen women interviewed attended neither of the formally organised opportunities to find out about their children's learning – but not because they were disinterested in their children's education. In fact most of them wanted advice about helping their children to learn to read and all were positive about their children's English literacy learning. These parents missed opportunities to find out about their children's school learning because they did not share the language of the school. The school's attempts to involve parents at the school site worked for only some of the parents, those with the cultural resources (Corson, 1993) which rendered them more able or willing to respond to the school's initiatives. There was diversity among the parent group which meant that some of them were less responsive to the school's initiatives to involve them.

The Bangladeshi women's group

At the time the interviews were held the school had just initiated a weekly meeting of a group of Bangladeshi women in the 'parents' room', in a mobile classroom in the school's playground. One of the organisers of the group was Naim's mother, who said, 'We have just started a group for Bengali women'. When asked about its rationale, Naim's mother said it was to 'get the mums to come into a group, I think this would be very useful'. The group had been organised, she said, by a teacher with responsibility for community links in the school. But of the women interviewed, only Sultanas' mother attended the group, and then 'only sometimes'. None of the other sixteen had been. Aminur's mother said 'I can't go, I have my housework', while Taslima's mother, who had recently moved to the area, said 'I used to go at the other school, but not since we came to this area' . Of the other women, only Husna's mother articulated her reasons for not attending the women's group:

I'm a bit embarrassed going to them because I can't really get on with them, not knowing the language

Although the group had been set up specifically for Bangladeshi women, Husna's mother did not feel confident to attend. To explain, she focused on the difference between her cultural resources and the expectations of the school. She spoke the same language as the other Bangladeshi parents in the school but perceived that as the women's group was located in the school, it was part of the school's dominant-language domain. Although it was early days for the Bangladeshi women's group, the women in the present study reacted with little enthusiasm to its development. Here is further evidence of the school's attempts to involve the parents at the school site – and again the mothers' responses suggest that the teachers were not reaching them with this initiative.

Informal parent-teacher communication

The teachers said that they took advantage of informal opportunities to communicate with the children's parents, for example at the beginning and end of the school day when children were brought to and collected from school. One of the teachers suggested that this was easier for teachers to achieve when children were younger, when parents 'are very keen'. This teacher suggested that the 'early years' teachers made a particular effort to talk to the parents in informal contexts:

The Reception teachers are good because they will spend time with them at the end of the day, beginning of the day, talking to them about their books

Another teacher spoke about Hussain Ali's father's positive attitude to reading support, who would 'come and show me the books he's purchasing, asking me if they're relevant'. This reflected the teachers' view that the parents were positive about supporting their children's reading. The teachers spoke about the parents who seemed more responsive to their initiatives, suggesting that 'younger parents' who had been educated in Britain were more responsive to the school's initiatives to involve them.

The teachers' view that the most interested parents were those who had been educated in Britain may go some way to explaining the difference between the teachers' generally positive comments about informal parent-teacher contacts, and the less positive responses of the parents. Of the eleven women who commented on informal opportunities to communicate with their children's teachers, Dilwar's mother and Joyghun's mother indicated that they would be able to approach the teacher if necessary, although there was no evidence that either had actually done so. Of the remainder, six parents suggested that the main reason that they could not ask the teachers for information or advice about their children's literacy learning was that they were not proficient in the teachers' language. For example, Mahbubur's mother said she could not ask her son's teacher for help 'because I can't speak the language'. Muhitur's mother's response seemed to indicate that she would welcome the chance to speak to her child's teacher but wasn't certain whether an interpreter would be available:

> If I found someone there who was a Bengali interpreter I would definitely go and talk to the teacher

When asked whether there was an interpreter at the school, Muhitur's mother replied 'I don't know'. These responses indicate that the main difficulty for these parents in communicating with their child's teacher was the difference between their language and that accepted by the school. Husna's mother described the experience of attempting to speak to her daughter's teacher:

> I asked once before but again because I don't know the language or read and write I felt embarrassed and couldn't understand, because my husband was in Bangladesh as well, that was a long time ago

Husna's mother articulated her inability to speak to the teacher about Husna's learning in terms of the school's accepted language and her own inability to use or understand it. Sultanas' mother considered that the teachers did not give her any information because they thought that she was unable to support her daughter's literacy learning: 'I think because I don't understand English they don't ask me to help'. The Bangladeshi women's responses build up a picture of parents who were willing to speak to their children's teachers but were disempowered by the difference between the language accepted and used by the school, and their own.

Yet it is also a picture of a school which sought to communicate with minority-language parents through a range of initiatives, including parents' evenings, parents' workshops, a Bangladeshi women's group, and other informal opportunities at the school site. Valley Community Primary School was doing more than most schools to communicate with and involve the parents of minority-language children. Interpreters were sometimes provided for parents' evenings, parents were invited into the classroom to learn about the school curriculum, teachers said that they made themselves available to parents at the beginning and end of the school day, and a Bangladeshi women's group had been initiated on the school grounds. Notwithstanding these initiatives, however, there were some parents who felt that they did not have access to their children's teachers or to information about their children's schooling. A symptom of their need for better communication with the school was their frustration that they were unable to contribute to their children's reading of school books.

What schools can do

Schools can become more effective in their efforts to involve minority-language parents in their children's school learning when they use the parents' languages and literacies as the means of communication; when teachers are easily available to parents; when the environment of the school is welcoming everyone in the community; and when the school invests sufficient resources in the process of parental involvement.

Interpreters and communication between parents and teachers

A crucial issue for schools in communicating with minority-language parents is the provision of appropriate interpreters. First there must be a linguistic match: the person employed to interpret must speak the same language as the parent. There have been a number of instances of support staff being employed by schools on the basis that they speak the same Asian language as the children and their families (or even that they claim to speak *all* Asian languages), when in fact their competence is in a language quite different from that of most of the children in the school. For example, an interpreter may speak the standard Urdu of the educated (Pakistani) group, while the parents (and children) speak a regional Pakistani language, such as Mirpuri, Pushto or Hindko. It is important that Head Teachers and appointment panels ensure that a governor who speaks minority Asian languages participates in the selection process on such occasions. A key point here is that all school staff should know which languages are spoken by which families so that appropriate interpreters can be found.

Secondly, an interpreter who speaks the same language as the families of many of the children may still be inappropriate. The remark by Husna's mother about the Sylheti interpreter at parents' workshops at Valley Community Primary School ('It doesn't look right, the girl is young') revealed that the interpreter was not regarded by the parent as the appropriate person to interpret for married women. In fact, a number of the Bangladeshi women in the study initially refused to participate when I approached them through this eighteen-year-old interpreter. Only when I switched to Mrs Miah were they more responsive, as Mrs Miah was, like them, a married woman with young children in the school.

An interpreter used on an *ad hoc* basis may be inappropriate for other reasons. For example, parents are unlikely to want to discuss sensitive issues about their children's schooling in front of their neighbours. Most parents prefer to maintain confidentiality when discussing sensitive matters of, for example, attainment or behaviour, which are often the focus of teachers' conversations with parents. Yet schools will sometimes use the nearest convenient bilingual parent to interpret in a discussion about a child.

A third issue concerning interpreters is training. It should not be assumed that a bilingual person has the skills required for interpretation simply because of that bilingualism (Harman, 1994). For many schools, the logistics of staffing budgets dictate that the person called on to interpret between teachers and minority-language parents is a bilingual classroom assistant (learning support assistant). Such school personnel are invaluable in providing a bridge between home and school in multilingual contexts but it is important that the interpreting role is properly recognised and rewarded, and that bilingual staff are provided with professional development opportunities to ensure that they are trained (Mills, 1994; Martin-Jones, 1995). Otherwise the role of interpreter becomes an onerous addition to existing responsibilities and can too easily be taken for granted. The role of the interpreter, then, is crucial in supporting the efforts of schools as they try to open lines of communication between home and school. Many studies, including this one, have found that the school's reliance on English as the medium of communication has prevented parents from becoming involved at the school. Interpreters can be effective in facilitating the involvement of parents when they are appropriate in terms of their languages and status, when they are properly trained, and when they are rewarded for their services.

Written communication between school and home

A second aspect of schools' attempts to communicate with parents is the practice of sending letters home with children. It is vital that teachers have a good knowledge of which parents are literate in which languages. Letters can then be written in both English and the appropriate literate language of the parents. For many Asian families in British schools the spoken language of the home will not be the same as the literate language. For example, Pakistani parents literate in Urdu (and, in all likelihood, Qur'anic Arabic) may speak a language which does not have a written form. As with interpreting skills, school colleagues' skills of translation should not be taken for granted. Training should be provided where necessary; skills should be duly rewarded and accounted for in work schedules, rather than added to existing duties. Schools should also be aware that some parents are not literate in any language. For example, one of the parents in my study (Husna's mother) never attended school as a child, as her village in Bangladesh was too far from the school . She was aware that Husna's school had tried to communicate with her, but she had no clear idea of what the message had been:

> they haven't really said anything to me but Husna does have some kind of special lesson for her reading and they gave me a letter , but because I couldn't read it the children just read it themselves and it said something about a special class for Husna to learn to read

This response makes visible the difficulties of communicating effectively with parents when only using written means. If the teachers had known that Husna's mother was unable to read English (or any other language) they would no doubt have arranged to meet with her, with an appropriate interpreter, either at the school or at home. The school did try to inform her about her child's reading difficulties, and to detail their efforts to offer additional support but because she could not read the English letter, she was unable to become involved in a crucial aspect of her daughter's education. When I asked why she didn't go to the school to find out what the teachers had been trying to communicate to her, she said 'I'm a bit frightened because I won't be able to do it'. While the school had undoubtedly attempted to discharge its duty in informing this mother of her daughter's reading difficulties, she ultimately had only a vague sense of Husna's progress. Despite the teachers' best efforts, Husna's mother was effectively excluded from knowledge about a crucial area of Husna's education, because she was unable to read the letter sent home from school. This instance clearly shows the relationship between literacy and power in the process of schooling and parental involvement.

Minority-language teachers

A third aspect of schools' efforts to communicate with parents in multilingual contexts is the extent to which teachers of the same cultural and linguistic heritage as the families are employed. Although it is not possible to guarantee that all families will encounter a teacher from their particular cultural and linguistic background, employing teachers who share the heritage of the school's community is likely to diminish the parents' perception of the school as a domain which is separate and alien. In my study the Bangladeshi women consistently spoke of their feelings of remoteness from the school, implying that they saw the school as a 'white, British' institution. Training and recruiting qualified teachers who share the heritage of the school's population is likely to have the effect of closing the gap between the (usually) 'white, middle-class' culture of teachers and the minority-cultures of many of the families served by the schools. Again, however, a note of caution is needed. School managers have a responsibility to ensure that minority-culture teachers share the same opportunities for career development as others (Osler, 1994). Also, it should not be assumed that minority-culture teachers have been trained to use their cultural or linguistic resources in the classroom. As teacher education programmes are increasingly prescribed by government agencies, less and less attention may be paid to ways in which minority teachers can make use of their particular resources in the classroom. Head Teachers need to find out whether initial teacher education courses have equipped new minority-culture teachers to use their languages and heritage and if not, set up a programme of professional development (and subsequent appropriate reward).

Teachers' availability to parents

In my study at Valley Community Primary School, the teachers believed that they were available to talk to parents and that all or most of the parents were aware of this, but the parents did not feel that they could meet the teachers at the beginning or end of the school day. There was a considerable mismatch between the teachers' and parents' views of this opportunity for communication. This finding suggests that teachers should be as explicit as possible in stating when they will be available to parents. For parents whose cultural and linguistic background is similar to those of their children's teachers, it is difficult enough to enter the school domain and demand the attention of a busy teacher. For minority-language parents it is particularly daunting. So it might be necessary to adopt planned strategies to help minority-language parents feel more confident about entering the domain of the school. Ideally, teachers would be available to talk confidentially to any parent, with the support of a trained and appropriate interpreter, at the beginning and end of each school day. But this is probably an unrealistic goal, as school budgets for interpreters are finite and teachers often have to attend meetings at the end of the teaching day. A more realistic strategy may be to inform parents that teachers will be available at specified times, on particular days, so that teachers and parents are certain that an appropriate interpreter will be available, that time will be set aside for meaningful dialogue, and that confidentiality will be guaranteed.

A multilingual, multicultural environment

The physical environment of the school will send clear messages to minority-language parents about the institution's attitudes and ethos. Although 'multicultural' displays, notices and labels may be surface features, many minority-language parents will be encouraged to enter a school environment which welcomes them in different languages, celebrates the range of cultures of the local area and provides relevant information in a variety of appropriate languages and scripts. The ethos of the school is created by far more than its physical appearance but a first impression which presents the school as one which values and welcomes people of all cultural and linguistic backgrounds may make the difference between a parent entering the school site or retreating from it. And again, school managers need to reward those who use their skills to create such an environment. It should not be assumed that the 'Asian classroom assistant' will write labels in Urdu for every classroom on top of her or his usual duties. A second issue here is that of quality. In some schools labels for displays are written in community languages by children, sometimes incorrectly. When these stand alongside large, teacher (or computer)-produced English labels, thay can make the minority language look second-rate. It is also important to avoid doing what a well-meaning teacher discovered that she had done, when one of the parents pointed out to her that the Bengali labels on her mural were displayed upside-down!

A multicultural, multilingual curriculum

It is not my intention in this chapter to enter the debate about what constitutes a 'multicultural' curriculum. However, it is worth mentioning the importance of a curriculum which responds to the diversity of society and societies, as the curriculum is another aspect of the school which creates its ethos, and minority parents may be more likely to involve themselves in their children's schooling when the school's ethos has a positive orientation to diversity. At a time when the primary school curriculum is increasingly dictated by the centre, teachers may feel that they have enough to do in keeping up with SATs, OFSTED inspections, government initiatives and other external pressures, without having to concern themselves with developing a curriculum which prepares children for life in an increasingly diverse and mobile society. But social justice dictates that teachers' responsibility is to develop children's learning to the limit of its potential, and to teach them to think critically about their world. The curriculum will be more likely to fulfil these imperatives when it promotes not just a 'functional literacy' approach to teaching reading but also one which teaches 'critical literacy' (see Chapter One); when bilingual and multilingual skills are used authentically and meaningfully in the classroom; when assessment of minority-language children credits multilingual achievements rather than assuming that low proficiency in English equates to 'low ability'; and when teachers orient themselves positively towards the diversity in their classrooms.

Minority-language students are still over-represented in low-achieving categories (Cummins, 1996; Gillborn and Gipps, 1996). I argue here that one way to overcome this is through creating initiatives in schools which

counter the structures of power in broader society and enable all parents
to participate fully in their children's schooling. However, this is only part
of the argument. Parental participation needs to be supported by a curriculum which attends to issues of social justice, actively values children's
languages and credits achievement. Even in situations where conditions
are not favourable to such an approach, individual teachers can make a
significant difference in children's learning, thinking and development.
To quote Cummins (1996:236):

> Even in the context of English-only instruction, educators have
> options in their orientation to students' language and culture, in the
> forms of parent and community participation they encourage, and in
> the way they implement pedagogy and assessment.

School teachers are influential people in children's lives. In promoting
social justice and equality of opportunity in their classrooms, they can
make a difference in children's journey to becoming critical, literate
individuals.

Dealing with racist incidents

Racism in schools has been extensively discussed elsewhere (Griffiths
and Troyna, 1995; Macdonald *et al*, 1989; Massey, 1991), and is not
debated at length here. However, teachers' practices in dealing with racist
incidents in schools contribute to the environment and ethos of the school
and may determine whether minority parents are able to enter the domain
of the school. The report of the Macdonald inquiry demonstrated that an
'anti-racist' policy should cater for all groups and should characterise no
group as racists or victims. A generation of teachers may have had little
training in dealing with racism in schools. Two incidents came to my
attention recently, both at schools in the same area as Valley Community
Primary School. The first was reported to me by a Pakistani parent whose
nine-year-old daughter came out of school in tears, having suffered a
difficult day in school. She told her father that a child in her group had
asked her, during class, 'Why have you got shit on your face?' and when
she reported this to the teacher, she was told to ignore the child responsible for the taunt. Not prepared to let the matter rest there, the Pakistani
child insulted the other child and a brief scuffle ensued. When both
children were sent to the Head Teacher, they were disciplined equally, and

the racist language was ignored. The Pakistani parent immediately went to see the Head Teacher, where he was told that his daughter must learn to handle this sort of thing without over-reacting.

A newly-qualified teacher in a different school decided to introduce an 'anti-racist' theme to her teaching, in the wake of the publication of the report into the racist murder of black teenager Stephen Lawrence. As part of a lesson, her class viewed a television reconstruction of the murder and its aftermath. When the film came to the reconstruction of the murder itself, two or three (white) boys in the class said audibly, 'Go on, kill the fucking nigger'. The teacher obviously heard them but continued the lesson as if nothing had been said. In both these incidents the teacher concerned ignored the explicit racism of young students. It would seem that the teachers had received little or no training in how to deal with such incidents or lacked the confidence to do so. In both incidents all the students in the class, regardless of their own race, ethnicity or culture, would be given the impression that racism and injustice were permitted by their teachers. And the parents would almost certainly feel less inclined to enter an institution where they would feel that they could expect little support. Creating an environment and ethos which encourages minority-culture parents to communicate with teachers about their concerns for their children's education means more than putting up a 'Welcome' notice in several different languages. It means developing an atmosphere where social justice and equality are at the heart of interactions in and beyond classrooms, so that all students and their parents are valued in the school community.

Investing in minority parental involvement

I have already suggested that schools in multilingual communities need to make substantial investment in the involvement of parents. Schools in such settings will benefit from yet further investment in buying cover for teachers to be released to work with parents, rewarding those teachers who are effective in making links with the community, and employing teachers with a specific remit for involving minority-language parents in their children's schooling. In my study of parental involvement at Valley Community Primary School, the development of the parents' workshop required the employment of a supply teacher for two hours each week, to work with a class of children while their teacher teamed up with her col-league to run the workshop. This meant that two teachers could work with about twenty children and their parents (mainly mothers). The parents engaged in a range of curriculum activities with their children, including reading, viewing insects through microscopes, maths activities and so on. As we have seen, the parents who attended developed an enhanced under-standing of their children's school learning and some tried to emulate such activities in their homes. Although not all the parents attended, this was a successful initiative for those who did, and was possible only be-cause the school committed funds to the enterprise. In addition to buying in cover for those teachers who are introducing imaginative initiatives, school managers can support the involvement of minority-language parents by rewarding successful teachers who develop work in this area. As teachers are increasingly subject to review of performance, Head Teachers and governors can ensure that review criteria include evidence of working to involve all parents in their children's learning. Some schools have created structures which allow teachers to be promoted to posts which give them responsibility for community involvement. Teachers are more likely to commit themselves to go the extra mile to involve 'hard-to-reach' parents when they can see rewards other than those intrinsic to their vocation. School managers can provide this motiva-tion through investment in a viable promotion structure linked to com-munity involvement.

Community activities on the school site

Many schools have tried to bridge the evident divide between school and minority parents by providing community activities at the school site. Al-though the Bangladeshi women's group reported in my study had not really taken off at the time of data collection, it is this sort of initiative that can attract minority-language parents to the school site. Other schools have initiated, for example, English classes for minority-language speakers, which focus on reading for school purposes or adult-education oriented English skills. Less commonly, the school might provide classes in community literacies at the school site, for example classes in Urdu or Bengali for adults, perhaps up to GCSE level. For many Asian groups in Britain, literacy in the community language has strong associations with cultural identity, yet parents may not be as proficient in them as they would like. Many of the parents in my study had attended school for as little as five years, while a small number had no schooling at all. These women indicated that they would have liked the opportunity to become literate in Bengali. Other community activities may be negotiated locally by school managers, as they find out what minority-language groups require.

Summary

Schools can do a great deal to reverse the structures of power in society which prevent full participation by minority groups. Providing appropriate interpreters, teachers and assistants, making explicit teachers' availability to parents, creating a school environment which is visibly positive in its orientation to diversity, and investing resources in minority-language parental involvement, are all factors which will contribute to the increasing possibility that these parents will be able to participate in their children's schooling. However, these strategies to create a positive, collaborative environment for participation are very much based on activities at the school. In addition to making these changes, schools can build on the languages, literacies and cultural resources of its families. In Chapter Six I explore this area of literacy, power and social justice.

6
MULTILINGUAL LITERACIES AT HOME AND SCHOOL

Introduction

This study has highlighted the need for teachers to know which languages are spoken by the families of the children they teach and in which, if any, languages families are literate. We have seen that they need this knowledge to provide effective communication with parents, involve them at school and enable parents to contribute to their children's reading. This chapter considers a further dimension: how schools can build on the existing languages and literacies of the home. Collaboration between school and home in the education of minority-language children should not be one-way. As well as enabling families to become involved in the learning processes at school, teachers can build on the language and literacy practices of minority-language families, and incorporate them in classroom practice. The chapter begins with accounts by the Bangladeshi women at Valley Community Primary School of how they use languages and literacies at home, and concludes with the implications of these accounts for schools and their efforts to bring closer together the language and literacy environments of home and school.

Bangladeshi households as language and literacy learning environments

Data were analysed which referred to the women respondents' reports of, and reflections on, oral and text-related home literacy activities, and also to the teachers' perceptions of the Bangladeshi households as language and literacy learning environments. The teachers' advice to parents about supporting their children's English literacy learning is compared with the parents' self-reported literacy proficiency. The data suggest that the Bangladeshi parents were involved in literacy practices in the home and community that were initiated by the family rather than the school, such as learning Bengali literacy, functional use of Bengali, oral literacy activities in the home language, and learning to read Urdu and Arabic for religious purposes. Most of the data were from parent interviews, but there were also examples of teacher interview responses which indicated their knowledge and assumptions about Bangladeshi families' home literacy practices.

Storytelling in the home

I asked parents about oral literacy activities in the home and particularly whether they told stories to their children in Sylheti. In fifteen of the eighteen families the parents said that they told their children stories in the home language. Some told stories made up by the mother at bedtime, but most related traditional Bangladeshi stories with a cultural significance or Islamic stories with a religious message. In one of the families the father was the storyteller. Joyghun's mother's response to the question of whether she told her daughter stories in the home language was typical:

> JM yes, I tell Sylheti stories
>
> AB are they traditional stories, or stories you make up?
>
> JM some are traditional stories, others I make up. Some are Islamic stories
>
> AB how often do you do this?
>
> JM two or three times a week

This was clearly a regular literacy practice for this family. Other families reported similarly regular storytelling. For some families it was 'once or twice a week', others 'just when asked'. Rabia's sister reported that her parents told traditional stories to their younger children: 'like myths and legends, they talk about their mums' mums' mums, things like that'. These were stories located in the home country, telling of the cultural heritage of Bangladesh. Mohammed Ali's mother used home storytelling as a means of reinforcing moral and religious instruction:

MM I do tell them stories in Sylheti, but I tell stories in Urdu as well, about the Muslim faith, I also tell them not to be naughty at school

AB do you make these stories up yourself, or are they traditional stories?

MM I make them up, I make up stories based on my three sons, like 'there were once three princes and they became kings'

Mohammed Ali's mother reports that this storytelling had a religious and cultural significance in the family, since she used it for instruction as well as entertainment. And Taslima's mother reported that she regularly told 'Islamic stories that explain what Islam is, the proper stories'. For these families storytelling had a cultural, moral and religious significance which extended beyond learning to read for functional purposes, and beyond mere entertainment. Indeed, there is no indication that this oral literacy activity was perceived by the families as directly contributing to the children's literacy development. Storytelling was a family activity with a cultural value which was evidently not shared by the school. It is notable in the audio-cassette recordings of the parent interviews (and while they were going on) that the women responded differently to the question about storytelling: they were a little embarrassed and bashful and usually laughed with Mrs Miah as if the question about home language storytelling intruded upon a private family activity not commonly shared with outsiders.

This suggests that as in other minority-language communities investigated in different studies (Delgado-Gaitan, 1990; Anderson and Stokes, 1984), families engaged in a wide range of language and literacy learning activities which were not highly valued or even recognised by the majority-culture school. Stories told at home in Asian families are often located in the home culture and are endowed with cultural significance. Yet these stories rarely enter the domain of the school, unless particular efforts are made by the school to ask families to bring them into the classroom (Blackledge, 1994a). One of the teachers at Valley Community Primary School was aware of the 'strong oral tradition of stories' but assumed that it was diminishing, as fewer children talked about it nowadays. This teacher did acknowledge that

...perhaps we don't appreciate that enough as well, because that's an incredible skill really, to be able to tell stories like that, traditional stories

Another teacher acknowledged that a positive strategy would be to 'get parents more involved with the home culture'. The teachers understood that home language stories could be a valuable learning resource but they had not incorporated this activity into classroom-based activities. Story-telling as an oral literacy activity seemed to have a cultural and even religious significance which was not fully recognised by the school. Delgado-Gaitan (1990) reports family storytelling activities in Mexican families in California which had the apparent effect of enhancing children's cognitive skills. If the teachers of the Bangladeshi children at Valley Community Primary School had known that storytelling in the home was as vibrant and significant to the families as the children's mothers reported, they would doubtless have developed learning activities in the classroom which built on this activity. But they had only a vague knowledge that this activity was going on in the homes of the children so were unable to plan programmes of classroom work which arose from the stories.

Teachers' attitudes to oral literacy activities in the home

Other interview responses indicated that the teachers also made assumptions about the type and amount of talk in everyday family interactions in Bangladeshi households. One of the teachers spoke of a boy who was a high attaining reader and attributed his reading ability to his wide knowledge of the world. She thought that this knowledge had been acquired because the boy's parents talked to him regularly and believed that other children in the same class were less confident readers because the amount and quality of spoken interaction with their parents was relatively deficient:

Children who have no, don't seem to have been spoken to about where they, I mean the boy the other day was a year five boy, he hurt his finger and had to go to hospital and I said to him next day which hospital did you go to, he didn't know the name of it, now I would expect a parent to say we are going to Dudley Road Hospital and this is what's happening, just in general discussion

She continued with this theme, suggesting that children were not spoken to by their parents when they travelled to other parts of the country:

> they haven't known they've gone to Bradford or wherever they've gone to, and they don't know how long it's taken them and they don't know the things they saw on the way, and I think that reaps benefits when it comes to reading

At the same time, this teacher recognised the 'tremendous potential' for talk among the Bangladeshi families and acknowledged that some families had 'incredible amounts of conversation', and that the 'cultural structure of families' provided opportunities for familial talk which might not have been available to families with different cultural backgrounds. In such families, she said, 'you can see there's a high level of interaction, very high level in fact'. Nevertheless, she believed that the importance of talk in the family was 'quite a hard thing to get across'. There is a clear suggestion (which she herself said 'does sound a bit patronising') that the amount or quality of talk in the families was insufficient for children's learning. This view may have been based on the teacher's expectations of what parents should say to children, which may have been culturally con-structed. The families' language interactions were viewed from a mono-cultural perspective. The teachers seemed to position the Bangladeshi women as deficient in providing a language learning environment for their children.

Bengali literacy in the home

Parents were asked about their ability to read and write Bengali, about their English proficiency, and about their efforts to support their chil-dren's Bengali literacy learning. Of the eighteen women, twelve reported that they were 'very good' readers of Bengali and thirteen that they were 'good' writers (Table 3, page 73) – very different from their replies about their English literacy, when only Naim's mother said that her ability to read and write English was 'good'. Most of the women said that they were unable to read and write English, whereas only those who had never attended school said that they could not read or write Bengali.

The women's responses present a picture of parents who considered them-selves to be literate, but not in the language used and recognised by the school. It is already clear that the parents felt that they were unable to contribute much to their children's school literacy learning, possibly because they were not literate in the language of the school books their children brought home. Their evident literacy in Bengali seemed not to be regarded by the school as a learning resource. Aminur's mother made clear her frustration that she could not read the texts brought home by her son. When asked whether he ever brought home school books in English and Bengali, she responded:

> Only occasionally, but I would like more of that. I could explain more of the story, as it is I can't understand the English books

Several of the parents made the same point. Sultanas' mother spoke of her attempts to read with her daughter, 'I can't do it because I can't read English, but if it's a Bengali book I will read the stories to her'. Mohammed Ali's mother spoke of her younger child who was at nursery, where

> ...they give out books which have two languages, the Bengali at the bottom and the English at the top, I read to them now, I think that's a very good idea, I wouldn't have understood them otherwise, I think that's a very good idea that they are in two languages

There was no indication that these dual-text books were sent home with the children. What is clear is that parents understood that their Bengali literacy proficiency was a potentially valuable resource which was not recognised or accepted in the school. The school dictated that the academic, literate activity of those without power was defined as non-literate by the dominant group. The parent interviews show clearly that most of the parents considered themselves to be literate. In addition, almost all the women, including the few who were not confident with text-related literacy, engaged in oral literacy activities. The 'illiteracy' of the parents was assumed by teachers who valued and recognised only the dominant-culture literacy. In defining what 'counted' as literacy, the school constructed the Bangladeshi parents' lack of school literacy in deficit terms (Street and Street, 1991). The parents were not literate in English, the language of the dominant majority, and were therefore regarded as effectively 'illiterate'.

Bengali literacy, culture and identity

At the time of the interviews twelve of the parents were actively taking steps to teach their six-year-old children to become literate in Bengali. Like the Panjabi parents in Saxena's (1994) survey of the changing role of minority literacies in Britain, the Bangladeshi parents' efforts to teach their children literacy in the community language seemed to constitute a response to the threat of potential loss of minority language and cultural values. Hussain Ali's mother's response was typical of the parents who taught their children directly:

> As often as I can, if the children are settled, I will spend twenty minutes teaching them Bengali

Aminur's mother had a structured routine for teaching her children Bengali on Saturdays and Sundays. For some of the children Bengali tuition meant going to a class based in the school after the school day ended. This was taught by Naim's mother, and attracted Muhitur, Rahima, Belal and Mamun, in addition to Naim himself. The children attended one or two sessions per week. For other children Bengali instruction meant a private tutor coming to the house. Sultanas' mother said that a tutor was paid to come and teach her children four days each week, and the neighbour's children would also attend.

Six families were not at this time taking steps to teach their six-year-old children to read and write Bengali. Rabia and Husna would go to classes for this purpose later: 'about eight or nine years old, that's the best time to go'. Lilu's mother and Shopna's mother both expressed their view that it was important for their children to learn Bengali, although they were not yet having them taught: 'She should learn Bengali so that she can get by if she goes to Bangladesh'. Mahbubur had been taking Bengali lessons from a private tutor, but 'he's away, so at the moment they're at home with no-one to teach them'; and Joyghun's mother was surprised to learn during the interview that there was an extra-curricular Bengali class in the school: 'Are there Bengali classes in school time or after school? Do you know the times of the classes?' She returned to this question later in the interview, and was obviously keen for her daughter to attend. Aminur's mother also said that she didn't know there was a Bengali class, and asked whether the teacher would take her children. These responses suggest that the parents were very concerned that their children should learn Bengali, most of them from the age of six.

The parents talked about their reasons for, or attitude to, their children's Bengali literacy learning. Almost all were positive about their children becoming literate in Bengali. Their responses fell broadly into two types: parents wanted their children to learn Bengali for functional reasons, and for reasons of cultural identity. The most common functional reasons for wanting their children to learn Bengali were so that later they would be able to read and write letters to and from Bangladesh and so that they could communicate with people when they visited the home country:

> He should learn Bengali so that he can get by if he goes to Bangladesh. Also, letter-writing is important in Bengali.

Eleven of the mothers said that it was important for their children to learn to be literate in Bengali so that they could read and write letters when they were older. It might be argued that these parents were articulating more than functional reasons as communication with and in the home country would also be a cultural resource.

In addition, the Bangladeshi women spoke of the language as an aspect of their cultural identity:

> he will have to learn the language, that's very important, I value that very highly that he learns the language because we are Bengali, that's very important

Other parents spoke of their children needing to learn Bengali or they wouldn't know 'the language or the culture', making it clear that for the parents the language was a central force in cultural transmission. Sultanas' mother said 'She's Bengali, she has to learn, that's important', while Belal's mother insisted that 'They are brought up as Bengali, so they should learn Bengali'. Muhitur's mother said 'because we are Bengali, to us it's very important'. Aminur's mother indicated that Bengali had a cultural significance that was associated with religion, saying:

> When they go to Bangladesh it is a Muslim country and culture, so it is important that they know both Bengali and Arabic, so that's why it is important

These and other comments suggest that for these families the community language had a significance far beyond the functional, and that the language was a core part of Bangladeshi culture. For the Bangladeshi parents their children's learning literacy in Bengali was not merely instrumental, it was associated with transmission and maintenance of the home culture and an essential part of the culture itself. The considerable efforts made by the parents to teach or have their children taught Bengali suggested that the language carried a symbolic value beyond its functional use. For the parents, to learn to read and write Bengali was to *be* Bengali, hence their commitment to ensuring that their children learned to be literate in the language.

The parents' commitment to their children's Bengali literacy learning was also evident in their resourcing of Bengali literacy in the home. Half the parents provided Bengali reading books for their children. For four of the families trips to Bangladesh were opportunities to bring books from the home country which were not available in Britain. Joyghun's mother said, 'we went abroad some months ago and we got some books from Bangladesh'. For other parents resourcing Bengali literacy learning meant buying the instruction book for their class: 'the three of them have one each, for Class One'. This evidence of parents' commitment to resourcing their children's Bengali literacy learning contrasted with their attempts to resource the children's English learning: there were few English books in most households and none in others. However, the parents had a clearer idea of which books were appropriate for learning to read Bengali, as they had been told specifically which books to buy for the children's Bengali classes, and because most of them could read Bengali, they were able to select books during trips to Bangladesh. The parents' confidence that they had the appropriate texts for their children to learn their Bengali literacy lessons was very different from their uncertainty about which books were useful for English literacy learning.

Parents' attitude to Bengali instruction in school

A further indicator of the value of Bengali to these parents was their suggestion that they would like Bengali taught in their children's schools. Of the eighteen women interviewed, sixteen positively stated that they would like their children to learn Bengali at school. Exemplifying this position was Taslima's mother:

> Yes, we do want Bengali teachers at school, if there are any, it's not just my kids that need it, it's other kids, yes if there was a teacher I would take them to school, as long as they know how to read some Bengali, that's all right

Husna's mother was concerned about the quality of teaching of Bengali (in the after-school class), saying 'they are just messing about down there now, the Bengali teacher is on her own but if it was a proper teacher it would be better'. The overall opinion of the parents was that they wanted Bengali teaching in the school, either within or beyond the curriculum, even though virtually all the parents took action to tutor their children in Bengali in the home or community. These responses emphasise the parents' commitment to their children's Bengali literacy learning. They called for more time to be spent on Bengali at school and for it to be more strongly supported by the school. The parents' commitment to the cultural value of Bengali seemed to constitute a symbolic assertion of their cultural identity. In Heller's (1985) study of the use of English and French in the wake of legislation to bring about univeral use of French in Quebec, commitment to the use of a particular language clearly demonstrated its symbolic boundary function. For the Bangladeshi parents of children at Valley Community Primary School, language was more than a means of communication. It was invested with symbolic boundary functions and represented a reliable guide to eligibility for group membership (Dabene and Moore, 1995). For these women Bengali was beyond the knowledge or control of the dominant group and therefore its active maintenance represented the maintenance of the home culture. It may also have constituted a symbolic response to the domination of the majority group.

Literacy for religious purposes

Although the parents were not directly asked about their children's attendance at the mosque or about teaching their children to read Arabic or Urdu, many of them referred to these aspects of their cultural lives. Some sent their children to private tutors to learn to read the Qur'an in Arabic, while others sent their children to the local mosque. As we have seen, some of the parents considered that the children were still too young to go to the mosque: 'she's not old enough yet, you have to be eight'. Some parents taught their children Urdu and Arabic themselves, generally at the weekends when the children were not tired from school, just as for Bengali. Sultanas' mother employed a private tutor to come to the house four times each week to teach Urdu as well as Bengali. Aminur's mother said that her children were still too young to cross the road to go to mosque but, she said, 'I do try to get them to read the Qur'an'.

The parents were clearly positive about their children learning Arabic: 'they must learn Arabic because that is very important, that is Islamic law'. This attitude was not shared by the teachers. The question of attendance at the mosque was not raised in the questions put at interview, but one of the teachers commented as follows:

> Mosque does have influence on it because at the mosque the emphasis without a doubt is on reading without understanding, getting the words right or you'll be smacked if you don't get them right. This has a very powerful influence on them because that's what they have to do at mosque, it doesn't matter whether they understand or not, in fact they don't understand it, what they're reading, but you must get it right because if you don't get it right there'll be serious trouble. When they're reading Arabic or even Urdu I think in many cases they don't necessarily understand what they're reading

This teacher clearly did not share the parents' commitment to their children's learning of Arabic for religious purposes. Yet this learning was valued by the parents, and was a regular feature of many of the children's learning.

The oral and text-related literacy activities the Bangladeshi families engaged in were of cultural significance, such as telling stories in the home language which often referred to moral or religious themes. Most of the parents were literate in Bengali but were regarded as 'illiterate' by the school. Yet the families made concerted efforts to teach their children to read and write Bengali and they would have liked more Bengali to be taught in the school. Bengali was of symbolic importance in terms of their cultural identity. Some of the parents spoke in addition of their efforts to teach their children Arabic for religious purposes.

There was little evidence that the parents' languages or literacies were even acknowledged in the school curriculum. This meant that the teachers could not build on the language and literacy resources of the Bangladeshi families when they were teaching the children to become proficient users of language. It was as if the children lived in a world of language and literacy at home which was quite separate from that of the school. Research and practice demonstrates that children's attainment is enhanced when there is continuity in language and literacy learning between home and school. Continuity is provided not only when minority households function more like schools but also when schools make authentic, planned use of the languages and literacies of the home. So what can schools do to make use of languages and literacies which are unfamiliar to most teachers?

What schools can do

In Chapter Five I referred briefly to the role of curriculum activities in creating a school ethos which would encourage parents to become involved at the school. I now expand on the kind of classroom practice which can build on the language and literacy environments of minority-language homes. The approach to literacy teaching which I propose allows teachers to provide continuity and consistency in children's learning experiences at home and school. Such an approach requires teachers to plan to use pupils' existing cultural and linguistic knowledge, maintain high expectations of pupils while offering appropriate support, develop activities which are purposeful and meaningful to the pupils and to resource the curriculum with texts which are at once culturally compatible and critically challenging. In adopting such an approach, teachers will involve pupils in classroom literacy activities which engage with their culture, identity and understanding of their world.

Home languages and literacies in the curriculum

The statements by the Bangladeshi women that they regularly told stories to their children came as a surprise to the children's teachers. As we have seen, the stories were used not only as entertainment but also to transmit aspects of Bangladeshi identity, reinforce moral messages and consolidate Islamic understanding. In addition, the stories developed children's knowledge of narrative structure and the language of story. Children from a variety of cultural and linguistic backgrounds enjoy the experience of storytelling at home. Here is an ideal opportunity for teachers to plan for the linguistic resources of the home and community to be given a voice in the classroom. Although storytelling in the classroom currently plays a limited role in the curriculum, students' language and literacy learning will benefit from an approach which encourages children to re-tell the stories of their homes (Blackledge, 1994a). When children re-tell stories in homogeneous linguistic groups, not only is their home culture valued but also their home language. The stories can be presented bilingually by children, in the home language and English, through puppet-shows and dramatic presentations; older students can tell the stories to young children, further developing the language skills of both groups. Students can publish their stories in book form, word-processed, illustrated and bound, in the community language, in English, or in both languages. Parents and other family members can be invited to come to the classroom to tell stories to groups of children. They can also help with the re-writing of the stories in languages which use community scripts, as the teacher may be unskilled in this area.

In schools which are building on the language and literacy activities of their students' homes, the gulf between minority-language families and their children's teachers has narrowed, and an atmosphere of trust and collaboration has developed. Of course, involving a small number of minority-language parents in bilingual/biliterate classroom activities does not directly address the marginalisation of those who find it difficult to enter the domain of the school. But change can be effected by the simple process of saying to all students that their families' stories (and therefore their families' languages, cultures and religions) are valued by the majority-culture school. When the students and their families are cast in the role of expert for this kind of activity, and the teacher is cast as the one who knows least, the teacher hands to the student and the family some of his or her traditional power. This is one small step on the road to collaboration between teachers and communities.

Community literacies in the classroom

The Bangladeshi parents expressed their wish that their community language, Bengali, should be taught at their children's school. As we have seen, the women attached symbolic significance to Bengali, suggesting that to learn the language was a marker of Bangladeshi identity. Valley

Community Primary School had responded to the parents' wishes by allowing the parents' association to pay one of the parents to teach children Bengali in an after-school class, but children rarely used their minority literacies in the course of curriculum work. Children's and families' sense of the school's attitude to them will be affected by how teachers respond to not only their spoken languages but also their community literacies. The literacies of other minority groups are similarly associated with cultural identity. Yet these literacies will not enter the domain of the classroom unless teachers make planned, concerted efforts to invite them. Children who are biliterate may hide their home literacy from their teachers, despite the evidence that literacy proficiency in the majority language builds on literacy proficiency in the minority language. When students perceive that the sole language of the school environment is English, they will behave as though their sole language and literacy is English. When they perceive that their school is a multilingual, multi-literate community in which all languages are accepted and valued, they are more likely to demonstrate their proficiency in a range of languages and literacies. Teachers have the power to dictate where on this continuum their classroom is located. Even in schools where there is little will to develop and implement multilingual policy, individual teachers can indicate to children that their classroom is a place where all languages and literacies are valued.

This is not to say that minority literacies will be appropriate media for all, or even most, curriculum activities. The task for teachers is to design and discover curriculum activities which can develop children's use of community literacies. For example, a group of children might work on drafting and producing a school newspaper in several languages; a school brochure for prospective parents might be written in appropriate community languages; picture books for young children may be written by older pupils in the language of their community. Class assemblies to which parents are invited can be scripted by children and presented in the languages of the community. All of these (and many more) are activities for which use of home literacies is appropriate, and children who are literate in their home language will respond to teachers' encouragement to write in these languages in the classroom. These activities will naturally be most successful when students are supported by staff who share their literacies. When such support is available, students and their families will recognise that the school values them, their languages and their cultures, and minority-language parents will be more likely to become actively involved in their children's schooling.

Culture, meaning and classroom literacy interactions

Literacy teaching in schools can either affirm or devalue students' cultural identity:

> Literacy education, when it acknowledges the role of cultural identity, may serve to enhance self-esteem as it derives from a sense of self in a social context. (Ferdman, 1990:200)

The acknowledgement by teachers of cultural identity implies a teaching approach which is resourced with culturally appropriate materials, which encourages students to explore and define their sense of themselves, and which affirms their cultural identity and identities. However, affirmation of identity does not imply an uncritical, liberal acceptance of all cultures. Rather, it encourages students to reflect critically on their worlds and experiences. Literacy interactions which invite pupils to reflect on their experiences and which affirm their cultural identity create an additive dimension to their learning, which in turn increases motivation and attainment. When children see a writing task or a text and its symbolic contents as belonging to and reaffirming their cultural identity, it is more likely that they will become engaged in the learning task, and meaning will be derived (Ferdman, 1990). Teachers can carefully select texts for reading which are culturally appropriate for their students. Not that they should make assumptions about what constitutes a child's 'culture' but they should seek texts which have recognisable content. A key aspect of children's learning to become literate is the activation of prior knowledge in literacy interactions (Cummins, 1996). In learning to read an additional language, prior knowledge plays a major role in helping to make the new language comprehensible. Culturally appropriate texts will give students opportunities to bring to the classroom their prior learning, so that there will be continuity between home experiences and school learning tasks.

Minority-language students' sense of themselves can be further affirmed in literacy interactions when teachers have high expectations of them.

Children will become disinterested in reading if the task set for them is undemanding. Minority-language children can seem to be lower attainers than they really are, and this can lead to a mismatch between the literacy tasks set and the children's true potential to achieve. So challenging, demanding text-related activities should be set for minority-language children, with appropriate support available and in a context which is recognisable and familiar, to allow them to activate their prior knowledge. Reading materials should extend children's existing vocabulary and allow them to infer and deduce meanings from the text, while making connections to their world beyond the text. Once again, this process will be most successful where teaching staff are able to use both majority and minority languages to scaffold children's understanding. When children are given appropriate support, teachers' high expectations of them will enhance their sense of themselves as learners and develop their belief that they can become academic achievers. When students are consigned to the 'bottom group' because their spoken English has not yet developed, they are likely to stop believing in themselves as learners, with consequent risks of failure and drop-out.

A critical literacy approach to teaching reading and writing in the multilingual classroom

As we saw in the research studies reviewed in Chapter One, approaches to literacy teaching that focus only on the technical skills of reading and writing may be successful for some children in our schools but not for others, because they fail to address the causes of unjust relations of power in society. The teaching of reading and writing should encourage students to challenge the dominant group's construction of the cultural identity of the minority group. Cummins (1994b) speaks of a *transmission* orientation: in a transmission model of teaching, knowledge is imparted by the teachers and received by the passive learner. In a *critical* orientation, on the other hand, teachers encourage learners to engage in critical reflection on experience, and to address issues of social justice in society. Critical reading is characterised by questions which explore the social implications of texts; this level of interaction moves beyond the world of the text and reflects critically on relations of power in society. In responding critically and personally to text, pupils learn to understand and question structures in society as well as to comprehend the world of the text.

Critical literacy focuses on the potential of written language as a tool that encourages people to analyse the division of power and resources in their society, and to transform structures which are discriminatory.

How can this approach be implemented in the busy classroom, when more and more literacy activities are centrally prescribed? A key point here is the need to embed cognitively demanding literacy tasks in contexts which are familiar and recognisable to the students. So when introducing a new text to children, teachers can build on what they already know. This is more likely to be achieved when texts are carefully selected so that they are not only appropriately challenging in terms of their reading level but are also located in settings or thematic concerns with which the children are familiar. However, simply selecting appropriate resources will stop short of a 'critical literacy' approach. To engage students more fully with the texts they are reading, teachers can select books which raise issues of social justice and injustice. Teachers can then model critical questions in the reading process and invite children to ask questions of the text. Connections to children's own experiences and to other areas of the curriculum will encourage them to activate their prior knowledge in the reading process, and therefore increase their cognitive power (Cummins, 1996).

This is not to say that every text should be located in the children's neighbourhood experience. Rather, it is for teachers to support learners as they make connections between their world and the world of the text. For example, reading a story about a group of children who have no space to play in their crowded city can lead to students asking critical questions about the provision of play space in their own community. A fairy-tale with a non-traditional ending can lead to discussion about the positioning of women and girls in a range of media. An information text which refers to poverty in the developing world can lead to literacy activities which demand that children critically reflect on global relationships. Many texts provide opportunities for children to ask critical questions of their world. They will do so when teachers model critical questioning and plan activities which require children to ask questions. A further step in the critical literacy process is that of *creative action* (Ada, 1988). Having asked critical questions of text, it will sometimes be appropriate to suggest ways that children can act on their new knowledge.

I have reported elsewhere (Blackledge, 1994b) a project in a multilingual Key Stage 2 class which evolved from a teacher reading a text with children about a group of students in a South American country who wanted to make changes to their local environment. After brainstorming their response to the text, the Key Stage 2 children carried out and reported a survey of pollution in their area; they wrote formal letters to the Department of Health; they planned and wrote proposals for the use of a piece of wasteland close to the school; they read information books to find out about ways of improving the environment; they interviewed local residents in their home languages and reported back to the class in English; and they explained their proposals to the City Planning Officer, who carefully inspected their plans. A crucial element of these responses to the text was that children located their response in the real world. This was not an academic exercise: the children were meaningfully engaging with both the text and the world beyond it and in the process carried out a broad range of purposeful literacy tasks. This is only one example of the many ways in which critical response to text, and action based on that response, can become the heart of the primary curriculum.

Summary

This chapter has demonstrated that minority-culture families engage in a broad range of literacy activities which are often hidden from teachers. Bangladeshi parents reported that they frequently told stories to their children in their home language, Sylheti, and they attached great value to their children becoming literate in Bengali. If teachers are able to find out about the languages and literacies practised in the homes of their students, they will be able to build on them in designing classroom activities. When schools fail to incorporate families' languages and literacies in classroom learning, they miss opportunities to make connections to their communities, to provide continuity in children's learning, and to enhance their students' sense of themselves. A curriculum which makes planned, authentic use of children's languages and literacies and which teaches children to ask critical questions of their worlds can begin to reverse the unjust relations of power between majority-culture institutions and minority-culture families. In Chapter Seven I move from connections at classroom level to the broader context of involving minority parents in the development of policy and practice in schools.

7
INVOLVING MINORITY-LANGUAGE PARENTS IN POLICY AND PRACTICE

Introduction

We have seen that the Bangladeshi families of children at Valley Community Primary School engage in a range of literacy practices and events in their homes, many of which are unfamiliar to their children's teachers and are more or less disregarded as having no place in the English curriculum. We have also seen that the parents want their children to be successful at school and would like to support their children as they engage with school literacy learning. However, the Bangladeshi parents are often frustrated in this because the literacy of the school is exclusively located in the majority language. The minority-language parents would like to find out about their children's progress and about how to help them to learn to read and write English but, despite a number of school initiatives, they experience difficulties in communicating with the teachers at the school. This chapter considers the ways in which teachers position minority parents, often assuming a deficit perspective of their competence to contribute to their children's education, and asks whether teachers can adopt attitudes to these parents which enable them to become more positively involved in their children's schooling.

Literacy and power in multilingual settings

It is not only in the process of literacy teaching and learning itself that relations of power between minority and majority groups may be reproduced, but also in the attitudes and assumptions related to literacy learning. The majority group's attitudes to minority families' ability to contribute to their children's language and literacy learning in schools may maintain structures in society which prevent minority groups' participation in, and access to, other institutions of power. Majority-culture teachers may make assumptions about the behaviours and beliefs of members of minority groups that they explain from an ethnocentric, monocultural perspective. In fact behaviours and beliefs related to learning are not only likely to alter within and between cultural groups but they also interact in complex ways with aspects of social identities such as gender, culture, class and race (Eckert and McConnell-Ginet, 1992a, 1992b, 1995). When teachers assume that minority-language parents are in some ways inadequate for the task of supporting their children's academic and linguistic development, doors may remain securely closed, denying parents access to involvement in their children's schooling.

Teachers may assume that minority-culture families should organise their daily lives in ways which fit with the expectations of the dominant, white middle-class. For women, often the key figures in the home, this may mean having to make decisions about whether to adopt the cultural and linguistic rules prescribed by the majority-culture institution. To do so may mean putting at risk the maintenance and transmission of cultural traditions and identities; to resist may mean putting at risk their children's academic success. When schools build on the existing language and literacy resources of the home, there is little need for such decisions to be faced. However, for minority-culture families there is a high probability that if their children are to become successful in school literacy it will be necessary for them to learn and play by the rules of a game controlled by the white middle-class (Knight, 1994; Heller, 1992). In fact schools' attempts to communicate with minority groups about their children's learning may be contrived to inform them precisely of this: that in order for their children to succeed academically (and, consequently, in society), they will have to conform to and abide by the rules of the dominant group. Studying schools' attitudes to minority-language parents as literacy tutors makes visible the ways in which the dominant, majority group constructs the identities of minority groups in terms of their literacy, gender, culture, class and race, and the effects of these positionings in relations of power between dominant and subordinate groups.

Teachers' assumptions and expectations of Bangladeshi women and their homes

Some of the teachers in my study mentioned in interview the ability of the Bangladeshi women to create and care for home environments which were appropriate for language and literacy learning. These responses were located in the context of questions about the women supporting their children's reading. As one teacher said:

> in many cases mum's at home on her own because dad's either out working or out, you know, out, so there's a mother at home with five, six kids, now it's very hard to have time... who are you going to choose to be with and you've got often small babies, you know, incredibly busy people... I think reading is the last thing on their minds really, even though I think they're willing but it's just not possible

Another teacher saw things in a similar way:

> most of the houses I've been to are so incredibly fraught with things going on and children not necessarily behaving as well as they do at school

The teachers seemed to regard the mothers as having lives too 'fraught' with the difficulties of motherhood to even think about supporting their children's reading. However, as we have seen, the Bangladeshi women were generally very concerned about their children's progress in learning to read both English and Bengali and moreover, many created a structured environment in their homes in which to teach their children to be literate in Bengali. Far from it being 'the last thing on their minds', they regarded reading as a high priority. The teachers constructed for the parents an identity at odds with their view of themselves as competent caregivers. The teachers' positioning of the women in this way may have led them to have low expectations of the parents as home literacy tutors and potential policy-makers in the development of the school. At the same time, the parents may have accepted such an identity, in the belief that they were unable to contribute to their children's school literacy learning.

The teachers offered a range of reasons for the Bangladeshi women's apparent lack of involvement in their children's learning. They seemed to be aware that the parents perceived their lack of English proficiency as a difficulty in supporting their children's school learning. One teacher perceived that the women 'rely very much, certainly, on the school, because of their language' and another teacher said:

> They still think that being able to read the English is the most important thing and would feel that they can't be that helpful because they haven't got the spoken English and the reading of English

These comments indicate that the mothers' notion that they needed to be literate in English to support their children's English learning was seen by the teachers as a deficiency. But all the evidence showed that the school itself presented literacy learning as rooted solely in English, using English resources, so it cannot be surprising that the parents held this view. The source of the notion that English proficiency was required to support children's academic learning seemed to be located in the school.

Another teacher attributed the women's apparent lack of involvement in their children's learning to two factors:

> One there's an attitude it's inappropriate, it's the teacher's job, let the teacher get on with it, and not interfering. That's one attitude, which may come from home countries. The other attitude is, I want to be involved but I do not want to be put in a position whereby I am going to be embarrassed, and a feeling of having poor self-esteem is then compounded by the children adopting that as well

Another teacher agreed that 'there's the old idea of, you know, you learn at school, school is the place for learning'. This view is supported by evidence from Tomlinson and Hutchison's (1991) study of Bangladeshi parents' school-related literacy support practices, but the teachers' perception that parents regarded involvement in their children's learning as 'inappropriate' was not substantiated by the parent interviews in the present study. These Bangladeshi women would evidently have liked to contribute to their children's literacy learning but were disempowered by the cultural and linguistic structures in place in the school, and by the teachers' positioning of them as inadequate instructors in language and literacy. Typically, Joyghun's mother argued that 'If you get help at home and at school you do well', giving the lie to the teachers' assumptions that the women wanted to leave academic teaching entirely to the school. This mistaken assumption may have derived from the parents' disempowerment in the process of school literacy involvement. The parents said that they did want to become involved but couldn't because school-related literacy activities required them to be literate in English and to adopt the cultural rules of the majority group. The teacher's second argument, that parents would not become involved in their children's learning for fear of embarrassment, seems to recognise the disempowerment of parents in school-related activities. Their assumption that parents had 'poor self-esteem' may have been false – it may be rather that the parents appeared to the teachers to have little confidence or self-regard in the school setting because they were disempowered by the linguistic and cultural demands of the dominant-culture institution. The interview data suggest that the Bangladeshi women were confident of their role in the familiar environment of their local community, where their cultural and linguistic resources were accepted and valued. In Bourdieu's (1991) terms, the women possessed the cultural and linguistic capital to participate in their own community but not the capital required to become involved in the majority-culture institution of the school.

Class, competence and the professionalisation of teaching reading

The issue of 'class' also emerged in the teachers' assumptions about the mothers' ability to support their children's learning. When I asked teachers whether they tried to advise parents about how to support their children's learning, one replied:

> It's a class thing, isn't it, really, in many cases, and you're trying to make people have a set of rules which are really middle-class white rules, aren't they? In order for children to achieve in Britain today you've got to have those really

This seemed to assume that the Bangladeshi parents did not have the cultural resources to contribute to their children's learning. The teacher was assuming or perhaps accepting that the parents would have to learn to play by the rules of the dominant majority if their children were to succeed academically. She went on to say that parents had to learn 'middle class rules', because...

> that's how you achieve in this society, that's the way that society
> works, but you're not going to if you don't do it

Implicit in this response was the view that parents should change, to become like 'middle-class' parents, or risk consigning their children to
academic failure. There was no evidence that the school would consider
devising a 'set of rules' located in the parents' existing cultural or linguistic resources. The school view was reinforced when the teacher added
that the school was planning to lend school books to nursery children –
not for the children to read but for parents to read to them:

> you know, story time at the end of the day, because that's a very white,
> middle-class thing isn't it, reading a story before your child goes to
> bed? I don't think that happens

Implicit in these plans was an intention to teach parents the behaviours of
'white, middle-class' families so as to ensure the children's academic
success. The teacher had no idea that many parents told their children
stories in the evening. The teachers' remarks showed no intention of
building on the cultural or linguistic resources of the families. Instead,
they explicitly planned to teach minority-language parents to adopt the
rules of the 'white middle-classes'. Those who would or could not do so
would not 'achieve in this society'.

Further evidence of the teachers' construction of the Bangladeshi women
as inadequate contributors to their children's literacy learning emerged in
responses to questions about new initiatives in teaching reading and
writing in school. The teachers were able to talk extensively about modi-
fications to their classroom practice and developing strategies to teach
children to understand aspects of texts such as 'characterisation, motivation, empathy with the author'. They were concerned to ensure that children understood the texts they read, and that they learned to read using a
range of skills. There was firm evidence of such strategies in the teachers'
interventions in classroom literacy interactions. When asked whether the
parents could be involved, however, the teachers were less positive:

> Whether you could involve parents in doing that I don't know because
> it's taken me a lot of training, I've had to re-learn how to teach
> reading.

In a way you've got to get consistency amongst the teachers before you start thinking that deeply about parents doing it because there's inconsistencies among teachers

The teachers' responses seemed to indicate that they viewed the teaching of reading as a task for professionals, which parents could not attempt. They believed that specialist knowledge and skills were required to contribute to children's literacy learning – reading was a matter for professionals, who were more likely to adopt 'correct' methods (Vincent, 1996). It was best left to teachers because it was a complex, highly structured process. The clear implication, once again, is that the teachers did not consider that the mothers had the cultural resources required. As before, there were tensions between the teachers' positioning of the women and the women's own positioning of themselves as competent teachers of community literacies. By adopting a deficit view of the children's parents as potential literacy tutors, the teachers seemed to imply that the parents could not become active participants in their children's schooling. Yet schools can adopt a positive attitude to minority parents' ability to support their children's learning, as the following strategies for teachers indicate.

What schools can do

Teachers and educational policy-makers can create the conditions in which collaboration and participation lead to the empowerment of minority-language parents but first the rules of participation must be changed so that minority groups are no longer required to adopt the cultural and linguistic structures of the majority group. Many minority parents are not able to meet the demands and expectations of the dominant group and others may recognise that they have to risk aspects of their own cultural identity in order to play by the rules of the majority. When schools instead build on the cultural and linguistic patterns of minority groups, identifying strengths rather than assuming that parents are unable to participate, the usual structures of power in society can be reversed. Schools need to listen to the parents of the children they teach and to develop participation structures which build on what parents can already do. Crucially, teachers need to *believe* in the contribution that parents can make not only to their children's learning but also to the development of school policy. When this orientation to minority parents is in place, the process of parental participation in their children's schooling can be one of empowerment rather than frustration.

Listening to parents

Delgado-Gaitan (1996) describes a school initiative in a minority-language (Latino) context in California which was based on the reasons parents gave about their inability to participate in their children's school literacy learning. The parents spoke initially to a researcher who interviewed them in their homes and later in organised parent meetings. They said that they were unable to support their children because they did not speak or read English, because they were afraid to go to the school to talk to teachers, and because they had little understanding of the teachers' expectations of them. In some minority communities it is necessary to make particular efforts to enable parents to express their concerns. We have seen that the Bangladeshi parents at Valley Community Primary School did not feel that they were able to express their concerns to teachers, despite the school's efforts to create opportunities for communication. In fact, some of the Bangladeshi women were reluctant about expressing their concerns to the teachers even when they had the opportunity, as exemplified by a mother who spoke of her worries about her daughters' schooling:

> I don't want to complain and get into trouble, but Sultanas and Beauty, their writing is not very clear, they are not writing properly, in handwriting and reading they are not making much progress

Sultanas' mother would have liked to challenge the teachers about their teaching of her children but she seemed to fear the possible consequences. Although she, like others, was prepared to tell the researcher, she did not feel able to say the same to her children's teachers. Teachers need to assure parents that there will be no adverse consequences if they express their concerns about their children's schooling before they will gain their trust. We know that most of the Bangladeshi mothers did not go to the school to avail themselves of the opportunities for communication with their children's teachers and in such circumstances it may be necessary for teachers to visit the parents at home. Head Teachers can ensure that class teachers visit the homes of all children in their class during the first term of the academic year by making this a mandatory part of home-school partnership policy. School governing bodies can support such a policy by releasing teachers from the classroom to make home visits. The vast majority of teachers will require the support of a trained interpreter or bilingual home liaison teacher when making home visits to minority-language parents, so adopting such a policy has resource implications. However, failure to make such an investment is likely to result in the continued marginalisation of the parents of some of the school students.

In Delgado-Gaitan's (1990; 1994; 1996) study, minority-language parents expressed their concerns about their children's schooling in meetings run by parents from the community, not by the school teachers. Moreover, they were not opportunities for teachers to tell parents how to support their children's school learning but forums for the Latino parents to support each other, learning from each others' experiences of relating to their children's schools and learning how to assist their children in their schooling. Meeting together *without* teachers, they constructed new ways of becoming effective partners with schools.

What, then, is the role of the school in such meetings of parents? Schools can still do a good deal: they may initiate the first meeting and perhaps provide a room for it; they may act as a medium of communication about the time, date, venue and purpose of meetings; and, most importantly, they can listen to and act on the concerns that the parents raise. It needs to be clear from the outset that the school will take the concerns of the parents seriously and that Head Teachers and governing bodies will be prepared to act on their recommendations. This structure cannot guarantee that all parents' concerns will be addressed, but it is one means of giving a voice to those who feel unable to express their concerns directly to teachers.

Identifying the strengths of the parents

When schools identify what parents can already do, rather than focusing on whether they are able to meet the pre-existing conditions of the school, they can incorporate these strengths into the structures they develop for collaboration. Asking parents to use their cultural and linguistic resources to support their children's schooling is more productive than asking them to adopt unfamiliar cultural and linguistic patterns. Although minority-language parents may not be able to carry out the literacy support practices that suit white middle-class parents, they may well be able to support their children's schooling by using their own language and literacy practices – so teachers will need to find out what these are. The teachers' positioning of the Bangladeshi mothers in my study came from a deficit perspective that is, as evidence shows (Vincent, 1996; McNaughton *et al*, 1992), not uncommon among teachers. A constructive approach would be to encourage and develop supportive activities for parents which fit with their existing cultural and linguistic practices.

Building on the existing cultural and linguistic practices of minority-language families

If there is no single 'literacy' that is superior to other literacies, the literacy of the school is no more or less valid than the literacies of homes and communities. Hannon (1995) suggests that this can lead to a dilemma for teachers:

> On the one hand we wish to listen to and to learn from parents, to respect their language and literacy, and we do not want uncritically to impose school literacy on families. On the other hand, school literacy is our business and it is self-deceiving to imagine that involvement can mean wholly accepting all families' literacies as a substitute for school literacy. (p 150)

In minority-language settings, the dilemma for teachers is whether to insist that minority families adopt the literacy of the dominant-culture school or to accept the literacies of the home and make no intervention in the parents' attempts to support school literacy learning. Neither position is tenable. To impose school literacy on minority families is likely to lead to frustration and disempowerment, and adopting a *laissez-faire* policy may leave parents confused about the expectations of the school. Gregory (1996a) was told by parents of Bangladeshi children in London that they could not help their children read the English books they brought from school, because they were not literate in English. Gregory (1996b) summarises these findings in terms of empowerment:

> teachers may well be asking Bangladeshi parents to do the impossible without actually explaining why they should do it. It is therefore

understandable that parents may feel disempowered or resentful at what is requested of them. (p 91)

Expecting minority-language parents to adopt the literacy of the school can cause them to feel disenfranchised and marginalised, unable to take an active part in the teaching of school-related literacy at home because they cannot read the majority language, and staying away from the school because they feel that they cannot do what the school wants them to. The teachers' positioning of the parents in terms of their culture, class and gender will contribute to the parents' view of themselves in relation to the school. When teachers believe in parents' ability to contribute to their children's learning, the parents will believe in it too.

As we saw in Chapter One, it is important not to characterise minority-language groups as the same or even similar. While some might be happy to adopt the cultural patterns demanded by the school, others may find it more problematic. Some groups more than others, and some individuals more than others, may feel that aspects of their cultural identity may be threatened, so may protect their identity by adopting a position which seems resistant to involvement with their children's teachers. Characteristic of such groups would be failure or apparent unwillingness to attend parents' evenings, teacher conferences or other opportunities for communication with their children's teachers. Hardman (1998) found that teachers of Cambodian children in Philadelphia often believed that these parents did not care about their children's education, because they did not attend teacher-parent conferences nor sign homework. Yet the parents themselves expressed concern for their children's education, and did what they could to support their children's literacy learning. Many other studies (e.g. Trueba, 1993a; Delgado-Gaitan, 1990; Vincent, 1996) demonstrate this gap between teachers' and parents' perceptions of the parents' attitudes to supporting their children's education. If the parents perceive that in order to become involved in their children's learning, they are required to adopt aspects of 'English' identity and risk casting off aspects of their cultural identity, they may be resistant to becoming involved. One of the teachers in my study spoke of a plan to inform the parents about the school's expectations of them as literacy tutors:

There are a lot of parents, particularly younger parents that have been educated in this country, and they're, say, in their early twenties, they have some understanding of the system and they do ask a lot of questions

we think that might be quite a captive audience and perhaps do a more formalised meeting with the parents.

The Bangladeshi women would be rewarded with support from teachers in the literacy learning process if they had been educated in Britain and had some 'understanding of the system'. This apparently positive statement implies that those who were born and educated in the home country were less interested in their children's education and lacked not only the appropriate language to find out about their children's English literacy learning but also the 'understanding of the system' that would equip them to ask suitable questions.

The Bangladeshi parents' invisibility at the school was not a deficiency – they all had cultural and linguistic resources which were valid in their home and community. But the school directed its efforts to involve parents at those who were likely to be most responsive and this approach is a potential recipe for increasing inequality. Parents who required most support in teaching their children to become literate in English might have been excluded from the teachers' interventions (Toomey, 1989) while those who already had some access to the school would be further empowered.

None of the women in my study were educated in Britain and, as we saw in Chapter Five, it was younger women who had attended British schools that the teachers positioned as able to be reached and taught the cultural and linguistic rules of the school, and not those who had been born and educated in Bangladesh. Mothers who presented themselves (linguistically and culturally) as being 'more Bangladeshi' and 'less British' received less support and information in the process of their children's schooling. Those most in need of support remained out of reach while those who had already adopted aspects of English identity were given support by the school.

As far as the teachers were concerned, strategies for teaching Bangladeshi children and involving their families in the process seemed to be based on a reconstruction of the families' ethnic identities:

it's to do with – not really thinking about second language learners but thinking about white people, white families

It was as if the reconstruction of the Bangladeshi families' identities as 'white families' would resolve the difficulties of communication and attainment which were causing frustration on all sides. Rather than finding out about the cultural and linguistic resources of the Bangladeshi families, and incorporating these into curricular and extra-curricular activities, the school would wait until the Bangladeshi families had transformed themselves into 'white families'.

A two-way process of collaboration

To move forward, a two-way process of collaboration is required. First, teachers need to learn from parents and children what literacy practices take place at home. These will differ in different minority-language groups, and in different households within each group. Martin-Jones and Bhatt (1998) show that a broad range of literacy practices is present in the lives of young Gujaratis in Leicester, including, for example, shared letter writing in Gujarati on Sunday mornings. As we have seen, the home literacies of young Bangladeshi learners are multiple, ranging from formal instruction in Bengali to cultural storytelling. When teachers are knowledgeable about the literacies in the lives of children and their families, they will be able to value them and design collaborative activities around them.

Secondly, when teachers send children home with school books to read, they must ensure that parents understand the school's explicit expectations of them as home literacy tutors and these expectations should be based on what the parents can already do. When schools demand that parents perform literacy activities which are beyond their capabilities or understanding, the result may be frustration and resentment. Home literacy tasks which are achievable for the parent and cognitively demanding for the child will fulfil the dual objective of advancing the child's learning and developing the parent's confidence and competence as literacy tutor. Opportunities should be created for parents to discuss the home literacy learning process in a non-threatening environment, through regular home visits, at parent-led meetings away from the school site, at teacher-led meetings at school, in family literacy workshops with children or in a range of other settings as determined by local circumstances. It is not a matter of choosing *whether* to build on the existing literacies of the home *or* to inform parents about what the school wants them to do – teachers should be pro-actively doing both.

Literacy and empowerment

When minority languages are valued and respected by teachers and schools, the community of minority language users can begin to develop their voices in relation to the majority group (Corson, 1993; 1994). As the language of the minority group enters the public domain of schooling, parents participate in the activities of the school to a greater degree and begin to believe in their voices in the process of initiating change. When communities use their own languages in the school domain to discuss what is appropriate for their children's schooling, they are more likely to articulate their true concerns. When minority-language parents speak and schools listen, a process of empowerment can begin. One of the key areas in which parents can make their voices heard is that of home support for school literacy learning.

At an individual level, empowerment takes place by building self-confidence in the interactions between parents and teachers. Empowerment through literacy extends far beyond the notion of minority-language parents feeling good about themselves and is not something that one group does to another (Delgado-Gaitan, 1996). Schools cannot empower parents but they can create the conditions in which parents' voices are heard and their concerns are listened to, in which action is taken and even those parents who were once most marginalised are able to initiate change.

> Empowerment principles state that people who have been historically under represented can organise and through a process of critical reflection recognise their potential and state their goals for access to resources, thus power. (Delgado-Gaitan, 1994:144)

Delgado-Gaitan (1996) has shown how schools can retain power and maintain the existing order of disempowerment through the school literacy learning process, or use it to allow power to pass from teachers to parents. The latter course requires a process of critical reflection and implies that both teachers and parents have the right and the opportunity to question existing relations of power in the literacy learning process and to initiate change. Both can, for example, raise questions about the process of reading school texts at home. Are the texts culturally appropriate – do they allow children and their parents to activate their prior knowledge in the reading process? Are the texts written in the language in which the parents are literate? Do the parents have a clear understanding of what teachers expect of them? Are the teachers' expectations of the parents realistic? Are there opportunities for parents to give feedback to teachers and to each other about the home reading process? Are parents able to ask teachers questions and raise concerns about their children's reading? Do the home reading texts provide opportunities for critical reading? When such questions are tackled, teachers and parents can share their experiences of teaching children to read, parents can become more aware of their role in the process of children's school literacy learning and more confident about it. More importantly perhaps, minority-language parents can become empowered at other levels, as the school shifts to accommodate and value their cultural and linguistic capital. When this shift occurs, parents may feel able to involve themselves in the management of the school, suggest changes to existing policy and apply for jobs at the school.

The Bangladeshi women whose children attended Valley Community Primary School were a long way from being able to become involved in the management of the school. They did not share the cultural capital required to enter the domain of the school, which was dominated by white, middle-class professionals. My earlier study (Blackledge, 1995) shows that when schools want the local community to be involved in their running, minority-language parents can have a real say in the schooling of their children.

One barrier to minority-language parents' involvement in the management of schools is that school meetings are usually held in English, but there is no reason why school governing body meetings, for example, should not be held in the main language of the local community – say Sylheti, Mirpuri, Gujarati – with interpreters available for the monolingual English members of the meeting. This strategy would immediately render a large number of parents in some schools newly eligible for membership of the governing body and their voices could be heard. Parents who had slowly become more informed about their children's progress at school and involved with their schooling would be able to take a part in managing the school. Once they are affecting policy on how their children are educated, minority-language parents will be empowered and able to act in partnership with their children's schools. In this way literacy learning can lead to a reversal of the usual relations of power and social injustice in society.

Literacy, power and social justice

My study set out to investigate Bangladeshi parents' attempts to support their children's school-related English literacy learning in an urban setting in Britain. In the course of listening to teachers and parents articulate their perceptions of home and school literacy learning, and by examining the process of literacy support in the home and classroom, certain aspects of the relations between dominant-culture school and minority-culture family became clear. For the Bangladeshi group, home and community languages and literacies were symbolically associated with the group's cultural identity. At the same time, the ways in which the languages of the majority and minority groups interacted in the school setting reflected the relations of power between the minority and majority group in society. The mothers' determination that their children learn to be literate in Bengali may have constituted a symbolic response to the cultural hegemony exercised by speakers of the dominant language. To learn Bengali was to be Bengali. The women invested precious time and money to ensure that their children acquired this symbolic marker of group identity, which would be of almost no economic value in British society. Their policy reinforced the linguistic boundary between dominant and minority groups and maintained the minority group's sense of its cultural identity by asserting Bangladeshi group identity. In a school and societal context where the dominant language was the major prerequisite for access to structures of power, the active and resourceful maintenance of Bengali literacy symbolised the Bangladeshi group's determination to maintain Bangladeshi group identity.

Second, it became evident that the languages and literacies of the minority and majority groups affected the granting or denying of access to structures of power. The women's linguistic proficiency in the majority language was evaluated at the threshold of power. If they were willing and able to acquire the language and literacy of the dominant group, they were granted access to the dominant institution, where they might even share the power of the majority group. If not, they were turned away from the threshold and returned to where their own languages and literacies had status and currency. For the Bangladeshi mothers, access to structures of power depended at least partly on free passage back and forth across the threshold between dominant and minority-culture domains. It may be that the Bangladeshi women understood too well that to learn and abide by the linguistic rules of the dominant majority would not guarantee them economic power. But their efforts to support their children's English literacy learning were frustrated by school structures which insisted on English as the language of literacy interactions. By these structures, the school acted as gatekeeper at the threshold to the dominant-culture school, and denied the Bangladeshi women entry. The consequence was that the women remained on the outside of their children's education and were disempowered in their attempts to support their children's English literacy learning.

Third, it was clear that relations of power were exercised by the school in ways that reflected the structures of power in society, and that these relations between dominant-culture school and minority-culture home had implications for social justice. The literacy interactions at home and school involving Bangladeshi children, and interviews with the children's mothers and teachers about literacy learning, provided a window through which to observe the relations of power between dominant-culture school and minority-culture family. A number of social justice issues were raised by the analysis of literacy interaction and interview data. The women in the study were not enabled to use their existing literacies to support their children's school-focused literacy learning but were instead regarded by teachers as illiterate and even culturally deficient in their use of language in rearing their children. The teachers' misperception of the women's skills and resources constituted a coercive exercise of power: only they had the power to decide what constituted 'literacy'. The school's attempts to communicate with the parents were usually conducted in English so the Bangladeshi women either avoided meetings with the teachers or received information from them at second-hand, sometimes from young children acting as interpreters. Informal contacts between parents and teachers were rare, because the parents did not possess the linguistic capital which had currency in the school.

The school did not adequately resource school-focused reading at home. The families had themselves very few reading books, but the teachers kept their better-quality books in school and sent home books of poor quality, sometimes at inappropriate reading levels. Teachers' attempts to communicate with the parents were designed to inform them that the key to their children's success lay in adopting the values and behaviours of the dominant group and that their own language and literacy resources were of little or no value.

Finally, the teachers targeted the most accessible minority-language parents with their support and advice, especially those who had been educated in Britain. In targeting those who were most responsive and already possessed linguistic capital which was relatively similar to that of the school, teachers extended inequality and exacerbated social injustice.

This book pesents the voices of women from a minority group in British society articulating their disempowerment in the home-school reading process and thus in supporting their children's English education. In a multi-cultural, multilingual society, individuals and groups gain access to institutions of power in varying degrees. When the institutions of the dominant culture construct social distinctions in such a way that certain kinds of cultural and linguistic capital are required to gain access to power, those who possess capital other than that prescribed become marginalised. Heller (1999:14) makes this point:

> those whose interests are best represented in institutions of social and cultural reproduction can leave aside others whose linguistic capital has failed to become valuable in the new social order. Those who find themselves marginalised are left to try to find a way in, to resist, or to bail out altogether.

At Valley Community Primary School, the Bangladeshi women made attempts to find a way in through the gates of the majority-culture school but when they found that their capital was not acceptable in that domain, they bailed out, inevitably collaborating in their own marginalisation and 'a process of social selection' (Heller, 1999: 273), and so remained powerless to support their children's schooling. Thus schooling in minority settings seems to reflect the relations of power between majority institutions and minority groups that prevail in broader society.

I have suggested that even in schools where there is a will to include minority parents in their children's schooling, some parents will continue to be marginalised because school structures mirror structures of power in society. But this paints too bleak a picture of schools' attempts to involve all parents in the education of their children. The future of education in multilingual, multicultural communities can be one of hope and optimism, as educators and policy-makers realise that schools can reverse societal structures of power between majority and minority groups. Rather than reproducing relations of power in which minority groups are marginalised and silenced, schools can create structures which enable minority-language parents to decide what is best for their children's schooling and to take an active part in developing policy and practice accordingly. This book has shown that change can be achieved when

- schools alter the relations of power in society which dictate that minority-language parents and their children adopt the cultural rules of the majority in order to participate, and instead discover and build on the cultural and linguistic strengths of minority families

- schools provide minority-language parents with access to their children's teachers by ensuring that appropriate interpreters are available or that teachers speak the languages of the parents, and that confidentiality is assured in teacher-parent relationships

- schools adopt a curriculum which values and supports minority-cultures, makes authentic use of minority languages and teaches students to question existing structures of power in society

- schools create the conditions in which all minority-language parents have genuine access to policy-making, so that parents can decide what their children really need from schooling.

Unfortunately as Heller (1999) points out, schools do not show us where the definitions of the value of cultural and linguistic capital originate, nor how these values interact with other institutions in society. Schools are only schools, and social justice for all requires economic as well as educational shifts. But schools do make a difference, and educators and policy-makers can begin to reverse the present structures of power in society so as to enable minority-language parents to participate in their children's education. The teaching of literacy at home and school offers one way to initiate change and bring about a more socially just society.

References

Ada, F. (1988) The Pajaro Valley experience: Working with Spanish-speaking parents to develop children's reading and writing skills in the home through the use of children's literature, in Skutnabb-Kangas, T. and Cummins J. (eds) *Minority education: from shame to struggle* Clevedon, Multilingual Matters

Adams, M.J. (1990) *Beginning to read: Thinking and learning about print* Cambridge: MIT Press

Anderson, A. and Stokes, S. (1984) Social and institutional influences on the development and practice of literacy, in Goelman, H., Oberg, A. and Smith, F. (eds) *Awakening to literacy* London, Heinemann

Apple, M. (1982) *Education and power* London, Routledge

Aronowitz, S. (1981) Preface in Giroux, H. *Ideology, culture and the process of schooling* Philadelphia, TUP

Ashton, C. and Jackson, J. (1986) 'Lies, damned lies, and statistics' : Or a funny thing happened in a reading project, AEP *Project* pp43-6

Au, K.H. (1980) Participation structures in a reading lesson with Hawaiian children: Analysis of a culturally appropriate instructional event, *Anthropology and Education Quarterly*, 11, 2 pp91-115

Auerbach, E.R. (1989) Towards a social-contextual approach to family literacy, *Harvard Educational Review* 59, pp165-181

Becker, H. and Epstein, J.L. (1982) Parent involvement: A survey of teacher practices *The Elementary School Journal* 83, 2, pp85-102

Blackledge, A. (1994a) 'We can't tell our stories in English': Language, story and culture in the primary school, in Blackledge, A. (ed) *Teaching bilingual children* Stoke on Trent, Trentham Books

Blackledge, A. (1994b) Education for equality: Countering racism in the primary curriculum. in Osler, A. (ed) *Development education. Global perspectives in the curriculum.* London, Cassell

Blackledge, A. (1995) Minority parents as school governors in Chicago and Britain: Empowerment or not? *Educational Review* 47, 3 pp309-318

Bloom, W. (1987) *Partnership with parents in reading* London, Hodder and Stoughton

Bourdieu, P. (1977) *Outline of a theory of practice* Cambridge, Cambridge University Press

Bourdieu, P. (1991) *Language and symbolic power* Cambridge, Polity Press

Bourdieu, P. and Passeron, J.C. (1977) *Reproduction in education, society and culture* California, Sage

Breier, M., Matsepela, T. and Sait, L. (1996) Taking literacy for a ride – reading and writing in the taxi industry, in Prinsloo, M. and Breier, M. (eds) *The social uses of literacy* Cape Town, John Benjamins

Burdett, L. (1986) Two effective approaches for helping poor readers, *British Journal of Special Education* 13, 4 pp151-154

Campbell, R. (1981) An approach to analysing teacher verbal moves in hearing children read, *Journal of Research in Reading*, 4, 1, pp43-56

Chavkin, N.F. and Williams, D.L. (1993) Minority parents and the elementary school, in Chavkin, N.F. (ed) *Families and schools in a pluralistic society* New York, SUNY Press

Clyne, M. (1982) *Multilingual Australia* Melbourne, River Seine Publications

Corson, D. (1993) *Language, minority education and gender. Linking social justice and power* Clevedon, Multilingual Matters

Corson, D. (1994) Bilingual education policy and social justice, in Blackledge, A. (ed) *Teaching bilingual children* Stoke on Trent, Trentham Books

Cummins, J. (1994a) From coercive to collaborative relations of power, in Ferdman B.M., Weber R.-M. and Ramirez A.G. (eds) *Literacy across languages and cultures* New York SUNY Press.

Cummins, J. (1994b) Knowledge, power and identity in teaching English as a second language, in Genesee, F. (ed.) *Educating second language children* Cambridge University Press

Cummins, J. (1996) *Negotiating identities: Education for empowerment in a diverse society* Ontario, CABE.

Dabene, L. and Moore, D. (1995) Bilingual speech of migrant people, in Milroy, L. and Muysken, P. (eds) *One speaker, two languages. Cross-disciplinary perspectives on code-switching* Cambridge, Cambridge University Press

Dauber, S. and Epstein, J. (1993) Parents' attitudes and practices of involvement in inner-city elementary and middle schools, in Chavkin, N.F. (ed) *Families and schools in a pluralistic society* New York, SUNY Press

Davie, C.E., Butler, N. and Goldstein, H. (1972) *From birth to seven: A report of the National Child Development Study,* London, Longman/National Children's Bureau.

de Castell and Luke (1987) Literacy instruction: Technology and technique, in *American Journal of Education*, 95, pp413-440

de Castell, S., Luke, A. and Egan, K. (1986) *Literacy, society and schooling* New York, Cambridge University Press

Delgado-Gaitan, C. (1990) *Literacy for empowerment* London, Falmer

Delgado-Gaitan, C. (1991) Involving parents in the schools: a process of empowerment *American Journal of Education* 100, 1, pp20-46

Delgado-Gaitan, C. (1993) Researching change and changing the researcher, *Harvard Educational Review* 63, 4, pp389-411

Delgado-Gaitan, C. (1994) Sociocultural change through literacy: toward the empowerment of families, in Ferdman B.M., Weber R.-M. and Ramirez A.G. (eds.) *Literacy across languages and cultures*, New York, SUNY Press

Delgado-Gaitan, C. (1996) *Protean literacy. Extending the discourse on empowerment* London, Falmer

Delgado-Gaitan C. and Trueba H. (1991) *Crossing cultural borders: Education for immigrant families in America* Lewes, Falmer

Department of Education and Science (1975) *A language for life (The Bullock Report)* London, HMSO.

Devine, J. (1994) Literacy and social power, in Ferdman B.M., Weber R.-M. and Ramirez A.G. (eds) *Literacy across languages and cultures* New York, SUNY Press

Eckert, P. and McConnell-Ginet, S. (1992a) Think practically and look locally: Language and gender as community-based practice. *Annual Review of Anthropology* 21 pp461-90

Eckert, P. and McConnell-Ginet, S. (1992b) Communities of practice: where language, gender and power all live, in Hall, K., Bucholtz, M. and Moonwomon, B. (eds) *Locating power. Proceedings of the Second Berkeley Women and Language Conference*. Berkeley, University of California Press. Reprinted in Coates, J. (ed) (1998) *Language and gender. A reader.* Oxford, Blackwell

Eckert, P. and McConnell-Ginet, S. (1995) Constructing meaning, constructing selves: snapshots of language, gender and class from Belten High, in Hall, K. and Bucholtz, M. (eds), *Gender Articulated. Language and the socially constructed self* New York, Routledge

Farah, I. (1998) Sabaq: Context of learning literacy for girls in rural Pakistan, in Durgunoglu, A.Y. and Verhoeven, L. (eds) *Literacy development in a multilingual context* New Jersey, Earlbaum

Farquhar, C., Blatchford, P., Burke, J., Plewis, I. and Tizard, B. (1985) A comparison of the views of parents and reception teachers *Education 3-13* 13, pp17-22

Feitelson, D. and Goldstein, Z. (1986) Patterns of book ownership and reading to young children in Israeli school-oriented and nonschool-oriented families *Reading Teacher*, 39 pp924-30

Ferdman, B.M. (1990) Literacy and cultural identity, *Harvard Educational Review* 60, pp181-204

Ferdman, B.M and Weber, R.-M. (1994) Literacy across languages and cultures, in Ferdman B.M., Weber R-M and Ramirez A.G. (eds.) *Literacy across languages and cultures*, New York, SUNY Press

Fishman, J. (1989) *Language and ethnicity in minority sociolinguistic perspective* Clevedon, Multilingual Matters

Fishman, J. (1991) *Reversing language shift* Clevedon, Multilingual Matters

Francis, H. (1987) Hearing beginning readers: Problems of relating practice to theory in interpretation and evaluation, *British Educational Research Journal* 13, 3 pp215-25

Freire, P. (1970) *Pedagogy of the oppressed* New York, Continuum

Freire, P. and Macedo, D. (1987) *Literacy: Reading the word and the world* London, Routledge

Ghuman, P. and Gallop, R. (1981) Educational attitudes of Bengali families in Cardiff, in *Journal of Multicultural and Multilingual Development* 2, 2, pp127-144

Gibson, D. (1996) Literacy, knowledge, gender and power in the workplace on three farms in the Western Cape, in Prinsloo, M. and Breier, M. (eds) *The social uses of literacy* Cape Town, John Benjamins

Gillborn, D. and Gipps, C. (1996) *Recent research on the achievements of ethnic minority pupils.* London, Ofsted

Giroux, H. (1987) Literacy and the pedagogy of political empowerment, in Freire, P. and Macedo, D. (1987) *Literacy: Reading the word and the world* London, Routledge

Glynn, T. (1996) Pause prompt praise: Reading tutoring procedures for home and school partnership, in Wolfendale, S. and Topping, K. (eds) *Family involvement in literacy. Effective partnerships in education* London, Cassell

Glynn, T. and Glynn, V. (1986) Shared reading by Cambodian mothers and children learning English as a second language: Reciprocal gains *The Exceptional Child* 33, 3 pp159-72

Glynn, T. and McNaughton, S. (1985) The Mangere home and school remedial reading procedures: Continuing research on their effectiveness. *New Zealand Journal of Psychology* 14 pp66-77

Golby, M. (1993) Parents as school governors, in Munn, P. (ed) *Parents and schools: Customers, managers or partners?* London, Routledge

Goldenberg, C., Reese, L. and Gallimore, R. (1992) Effects of literacy materials from school on Latino children's home experiences and early reading achievement, *American Journal of Education* 100 pp497-536

Gregory, E. (1996a) *Making sense of a new world. Learning to read in a second language.* London, Paul Chapman

Gregory, E. (1996b) Learning from the community: a family literacy project with Bangladeshi-origin children in London, in Wolfendale, S. and Topping, K. (eds) *Family involvement in literacy. Effective partnerships in education* London, Cassell.

Griffiths, M. and Troyna, B. (eds) (1995) *Antiracism, culture and social justice in education.* Stoke on Trent, Trentham Books

Gulliver, J. (1979) Teachers' assumptions in listening to reading *Language for Learning* 1, 1, 42-56

Hannon, P. (1986) Teachers' and parents' experiences of parental involvement in the teaching of reading *Cambridge Journal of Education* 16, 1, pp28-37

Hannon, P. (1987) A study of the effects of parental involvement in the teaching of reading on children's reading test performance, *British Journal of Educational Psychology* 57 pp56-72

Hannon, P. (1995) *Literacy, home and school: Research and practice in teaching literacy with parents* London, Falmer

Hannon, P., Jackson, A. and Weinberger, J. (1986) Parents' and teachers' strategies in hearing young children read *Research Papers in Education*, 1,1, pp6-25

Hannon, P. and James, S. (1990) Parents' and teachers' perspective on preschool literacy development *British Educational Research Journal* 16, 3, pp259-72

Hannon, P. and McNally, J. (1986) Children's understanding and cultural factors in reading test performance, *Educational Review* 38, 3, pp269-80

Hardman, J. (1998) Literacy and bilingualism in a Cambodian community in the USA, in Durgunoglu, A.Y. and Verhoeven, L. (eds) *Literacy Development in a Multilingual Context* New Jersey, Earlbaum

Harman, J. (1994) Towards empowerment: training secondary school students as community interpreters, in Blackledge, A. (ed) *Teaching bilingual children* Stoke on Trent, Trentham Books

Heath, S.B. (1983) *Ways with words: Language, life and work in communities and classrooms* Cambridge University Press

Heller, M. (1985) Ethnic relations and language use in Montreal, in Wolfson, N. and Manes, J. (eds) *Language of inequality* Berlin, Mouton

Heller, M. (1992) The politics of codeswitching and language choice, *Journal of Multilingual and Multicultural Development* 13, 1, pp123-42

Heller, M. (1999) *Linguistic minorities and modernity: A sociolinguistic ethnography*. London, Longman

Hewison, J. (1985) Parental involvement and reading attainment: Implications of research in Dagenham and Hackney, in Topping, K. and Wolfendale, S. (eds) *Parental involvement in children's reading* London, Croom Helm

Hewison, J. (1988a) The long-term effectiveness of parental involvement in reading. A follow-up to the Haringey Reading Project *British Journal of Educational Psychology* 58 pp184-90

Hewison, J. (1988b) Parental involvement and reading attainment: Implications of Research in Dagenham and Haringey, in Woodhead, M. and McGrath, A. (eds) *Family, School and Society* London, Hodder and Stoughton

Hewison, J. and Tizard, J. (1980) Parental involvement and reading attainment *British Journal of Educational Psychology* 50 pp209-15

Jones, K. (in press) Literacy, organisation and control: The literacy practices of work, in Martin-Jones, M. and Jones, K. (eds) *Multilingual Literacies* Amsterdam, John Benjamins

Jowett, S. and Baginsky, M. (1991) *Building bridges. Parental involvement in schools* Windsor, NFER Nelson

Jungnitz, G. (1985) A paired reading project with Asian families, in Topping, K. and Wolfendale, S. (eds) *Parental involvement in children's reading* London, Croom Helm

Karran, S. (1997) 'Auntie-ji, please come and join us, just for an hour.' The role of the bilingual education assistant in working with parents with little confidence, in Bastiani, J. (ed) *Home-school work in multicultural settings* London, David Fulton

Kell, C. (1996) Literacy practices in an informal settlement in the Cape Peninsula, in Prinsloo, M. and Breier, M. (eds) *The social uses of literacy* Cape Town, John Benjamins

Knight, A. (1994) Pragmatic biculturalism and the primary school teacher, in Blackledge, A. (ed) *Teaching bilingual children* Stoke on Trent, Trentham Books

Langer, J.A. (1987) A sociocognitive perspective on literacy, in Langer, J.A. (ed) *Language, literacy and culture: Issues of society and schooling* Norwood, Ablex

Lankshear, C. (1997) *Changing literacies* Buckingham, Open University Press

Lankshear, C. with Lawler, M. (1987) *Literacy, schooling and revolution* London, Falmer

Lareau, A. (1987) Social class differences in family-school relationships: The importance of cultural capital *Sociology of Education* 60 (April) pp73-85

Lareau, A. (1989) *Home advantage. Social class and parental involvement in elementary education* London, Falmer

Leach, D.J. and Siddall, S.W. (1990) Parental involvement in the teaching of reading: a comparison of hearing reading, pared reading, pause, prompt and praise, and direct instruction methods, *British Journal of Educational Psychology* 55 pp349-355

Lindsay, G., Evans, A. and Jones, B. (1985) Paired reading versus relaxed reading: A comparison, *British Journal of Educational Psychology* 55 pp304-9

Linguistic Minorities Project (1985) *The other languages of England* London, Routledge and Kegan Paul

Lytle, S. and Landau, J. (1987) Adult literacy in cultural context in Wagner, D. (ed) *The future of literacy in a changing world* Oxford, Pergamon

McCormick, C.E. and Mason, J.M. (1986) Intervention procedures for increasing preschool children's interest in and knowledge about reading, in Teale, W. and Sulzby, E. (eds) *Emergent literacy: Writing and reading* Norwood, Ablex.

Macdonald, I. *et al* (1989) *Murder in the playground.* London, Longsight

McNaughton, S., Parr, J., Timperley, H. and Robinson, V. (1992) Beginning reading and sending books home to read: A case for some fine tuning. *Educational Psychology* 12, 3 and 4 pp239-247

Martin-Jones, M. (1989) Language, power and linguistic minorities: The need for an alternative approach to bilingualism, language maintenance and shift, in Grillo, R. (ed) *Social anthropology and the politics of language* London, Routledge

Martin-Jones, M. (1995) Sociolinguistic surveys as a source of evidence in the study of bilingualism: A critical assessment of survey work conducted among linguistic minorities in three British cities, *Working paper series*, 13, Lancaster, Centre for Language and Social life

Martin-Jones, M. (1996) Enterprising women: Multilingual literacies in the construction of new identities, *Working paper series* 69, Lancaster, Centre for Language and Social Life

Martin-Jones, M. and Bhatt, A. (1998) Literacies in the lives of young Gujarati speakers, in Durgunoglu A.Y. and Verhoeven, L. (eds) *Literacy Development in a Multilingual Context* New Jersey, Earlbaum

Massey, I. (1991) *More than skin deep* Sevenoaks, Hodder and Stoughton

Matute-Bianchi, M.E. (1986) Ethnic identity and patterns of school success and failure among Mexican-descent and Japanese-American students in a California high school: An ethnographic analysis *American Journal of Education*, 95, pp233-255

Mills, J. (1994) Finding a voice: Bilingual classroom assistants and their role in primary schools, in Blackledge, A. (ed) *Teaching bilingual children* Stoke on Trent, Trentham Books

Minns, H. (1996) *Read it to me now! Learning at home and at school.* Buckingham, Open University Press

Newman, D., Griffin, P. and Cole, M. (1989) *The construction zone* Cambridge, Cambridge University Press

Newson, J. and Newson, E. (1977) *Perspectives on school at seven years old* London, Allen and Unwin

Ogbu, J. (1987) Opportunity structure, cultural boundaries, and literacy, in Langer, J.A. (ed) *Language, literacy and culture* New Jersey, Ablex

Osler, A. (1994) 'The flavour of the moment'? Bilingual teachers' experiences of teaching and learning, in Blackledge, A. (ed) *Teaching bilingual children* Stoke on Trent, Trentham Books

Powney, J. and Watts, M. (1987) *Interviewing in educational research* London, Routledge

Prinsloo, M. and Breier, M. (1996) Introduction, in Prinsloo, M. and Breier, M. (eds) *The social uses of literacy* Cape Town, John Benjamins

Reder, S. (1994) Practice-engagement theory: A sociocultural approach to literacy across languages and cultures, in Ferdman B.M., Weber R.-M. and Ramirez A.G. (eds.) *Literacy across languages and cultures* New York, SUNY Press

Saxena, M. (1991) The changing role of minority literacies in Britain: A case study of Panjabis in Southall, *Working paper series* 28, Lancaster, Centre for Langauge in Social Life

Saxena, M. (1994) Literacies among Panjabis in Southall, in Hamilton, M., Barton, D. and Ivanic, R. (eds) *Worlds of literacy* Clevedon, Multilingual Matters

Scribner, S. (1987) Introduction, in Wagner, D. (ed) *The future of literacy in a changing world* Oxford, Pergamon

Simich-Dudgeon, C. (1993) Increasing student achievement through teacher knowledge about parent involvement, in Chavkin, N.F. (ed) *Families and schools in a pluralistic society* New York, SUNY Press

Sneddon, R. (1993) Beyond the National Curriculum: a community project to support bilingualism, *Journal of Multilingual and Multicultural Development* 14, 3, pp237-245.

Sneddon, R. (1994) Supporting children's literacies at home. *Language Matters*, 1, pp23-26

Sneddon, R. (1997) Working towards partnership: parents, teachers and community organisations, in Bastiani, J. (ed) *Home-school work in multicultural settings* London, David Fulton.

Stierer, B. (1985) School reading volunteers: Results of a postal survey of primary school head teachers in England, *Journal of Research in Reading* 8, 1 pp21-31

Street, B. (1984) *Literacy in theory and practice* Cambridge CUP

Street, B. (1987) Literacy and social change: The significance of social context in the development of literacy programmes, in Wagner, D. (ed) *The future of literacy in a changing world* Oxford, Pergamon,

Street, B. (1996) Preface, in Prinsloo, M. and Breier, M. (eds) *The social uses of literacy* Cape Town, John Benjamins

Street, B. and Street, J. (1991) The schooling of literacy, in Barton, D. and Ivanic, R. (eds) *Writing in the community* London, Sage

Taylor, D. (1983) *Family literacy: Young children learning to read and write* Exeter, Heinemann

Taylor, D. and Dorsey-Gaines, C (1988) *Growing up literate: learning from inner-city families* Exeter, Heinemann

Taylor, I. (1998) Learning to read in Chinese, Korean and Japanese, in Durgunoglu, A.Y. and Verhoeven, L. (eds) *Literacy Development in a Multilingual Context* New Jersey, Earlbaum

Teale, W.H. (1986) Home background and young children's literacy development, in Teale, W.H. and Sulzby, E. (eds) *Emergent literacy: Writing and reading* Norwood, Ablex.

Teale, W.H. and Sulzby, E. (1987) Literacy acquisition in early childhood: The roles of access and mediation in storybook reading, in Wagner, D. (ed) *The future of literacy in a changing world*, Oxford, Pergamon

Tharp, R. (1989) Culturally compatible education: A formula for designing effective classrooms, in Trueba H., Spindler G. and Spindler L. (eds) *What do anthropologists have to say about dropouts?* Bristol, PA, Falmer

Tizard, B. and Hughes, M. (1984) *Young children learning: Talking and thinking at home and at school* London, Fontana

Tizard, B., Mortimore, J. and Burchell, B. (1988) Involving parents from minority groups, in Bastiani, J. (ed) *Parents and teachers 2: From policy to practice* Windsor: NFER Nelson.

Tizard, J, Schofield, W.N. and Hewison, J. (1982) Collaboration between teachers and parents in assisting children's reading, *British Journal of Educational Psychology* 52, pp1-15

Tomlinson, S. and Hutchison, S. (1991) *Bangladeshi parents and education in Tower Hamlets* London, Advisory Centre for Education

Toomey, D. (1989) How home-school relations policies can increase educational inequality. *Australian Journal of Education* 33, 3 pp284-98

Toomey, D. (1993) Parents hearing their children read: A review. Rethinking the lessons of the Haringey Project *Educational Research*, 35 pp223-36

Topping, K. (1992a) Short and long-term follow-up of parental involvement in reading projects, *British Educational Research Journal* 18, 4, pp369-379

Topping, K. (1992b) The effectiveness of Paired Reading in ethnic minority homes, *Multicultural Teaching* 10, 2, pp19-23

Topping, K. (1995) *Paired reading, spelling and writing: The handbook for parents and teachers* London, Cassell

Topping K. (1996) The effectiveness of family literacy, in Topping, K. and Wolfendale, S. (eds) *Parental involvement in children's reading* London, Croom Helm

Topping, K. and Lindsay, G. (1992) Paired Reading: A review of the literature *Research Papers in Education*, 7, 3 pp199-246

Trueba, H. (1989) Rethinking dropouts: Culture and literacy for minority student empowerment, in Trueba, H., Spindler G. and Spindler L. (eds) *What do anthropologists have to say about dropouts?* Bristol, PA, Falmer

Trueba, H. (1993a) Culture and language: The ethnographic approach to the study of learning environments, in Merino, B., Trueba, H. and Samaniego, F. (eds) *Language and culture in learning: Teaching Spanish to native speakers of English* Lewes, Falmer

Trueba, H. (1993b) Lessons learned: The healing of American society, in Trueba, H., Rodriguez, C., Zou, Y and Cintron, J. *Healing multicultural America* London, Falmer

Vincent, C. (1996) *Parents and teachers: Power and participation* London, Falmer

Vygotsky, L.S. (1978) *Mind in society: The development of higher psychological processes,* Cole M., John-Steiner, V., Scribner, S. and Souberman E. (eds.) Cambridge, Harvard University Press

Wells, G. (1985) *Language development in the pre-school years* Cambridge, Cambridge University Press

Wells, G. (1987) *The meaning makers. Children learning language and using language to learn* London, Hodder and Stoughton

Wolfendale, S. (1992) *Empowering parents and teachers: working for children* London, Cassell

Zentella, A.C. (1997) *Growing up bilingual* Oxford, Blackwell

Index

activating prior knowledge 123, 141
Ada, F. 57, 58, 125
Adams, M.J. 26
African-American 4, 50
African-Caribbean 17, 62
African National Congress 20
Afrikaans 20
analysis of reading interactions 69-78, 80-83
Anderson, A. 4, 25, 111
Anglo-American 4
Apple, M. 44
Arabic 15, 100, 110, 116, 118, 119
Aronowitz, S. 44
Ashton, C. 33
assessment 53, 103, 104
Au, K.H. 8
Auerbach, E.R. 4, 6, 25
Australia 15, 37

Baginsky, M. 24, 38, 51
Baltimore 48, 50
Becker, H. 47, 94
Belfield Project, The 30-34, 38
Bengali 50, 51, 63, 106, 113, 117, 121
Bhatt, A. 5, 139
bicultural research assistant 63-4
biculturalism 12, 51
Blatchford, P. 27
Bloom, W. 33
Bourdieu, P. 43, 44, 45, 131
Breier, M. 19, 20
Burchell, B. 50
Burdett, L. 33
Burnage High School 104
Butler, N. 26

Cambodian children 137
Campbell, R. 28
Chavkin, N.F. 50, 80
class
 – and reading attainment 6, 7, 25, 28
 – teachers' attitudes 101, 128, 131-135
Clyne, M. 15
Cole, M. 11
community schools 14, 15, 28, 50
Corson, D. 44, 45, 87, 95, 140
critical reflection 57, 124-126
cultural practices 2, 3, 12, 15, 17, 21
cultural reproduction 1
culturally appropriate texts 123, 141
Cummins, J. 4, 6, 10, 17, 18, 32, 44, 74, 102, 103, 122, 123, 124

Dabene, L. 117
data collection
 – school literacy observations 66
 – home literacy literacy observations 66
 – teacher interviews 68
 – parent interviews 67
Dauber, S. 48, 50, 94
Davanagari 15
Davie, C.E. 26
de Castell, S. 5, 6, 13
deficit view 19, 42, 114, 127, 133
Delgado-Gaitan C. 4, 7, 25, 40, 42, 45, 46, 56, 57, 58, 67, 80, 87, 111, 133, 134, 137, 141

Devine, J. 22
direct instruction 37
Dorsey-Gaines, C 25
dual-text books 86, 114

Eckert, P. 128
Egan, K. 5
empowerment 1, 2, 42, 45-47, 54, 56, 131, 140, 141
Epstein, J. 47, 48, 50, 94
equality 104, 105
Evans, A. 34

family literacy projects 57, 87
Farah, I. 15
Farquhar, C. 27
fathers and literacy tuition 51, 90, 91
Feitelson, D. 26
Ferdman B.M. 6, 12, 19, 61, 123
Fishman, J. 15
Francis, H. 39
Freire, P. 18, 21, 45
French 118

Gallimore, R. 54
Gallop, R. 51
GCSE 106
gender
 – positionings of Bangladeshi women 128, 137, 138
Ghuman, P. 51
Gibson, D. 20
Gillborn, D. 62, 103
Gipps, C. 62, 103
Giroux, H. 19
Glynn, V. 38
Glynn, T. 36, 37
Golby, M. 23
Goldenberg, C. 54, 55, 56, 83
Goldstein, H. 26

Goldstein, Z. 26
governors of schools 23, 105
Greek 15
Gregory, E. 5, 15, 50, 54, 84, 136
Griffin, P. 11
Griffiths, M. 104
Grillo, R. 28
Gulliver, J. 15

Hannon, P. 26, 27, 28, 29, 30, 32, 33, 34, 38, 69, 136
Hardman, J. 137
Haringey Project, The 30, 32, 33, 34, 38, 69, 136
Harman, J. 99
Hawaiian 8, 9
hearing children read
– analysis of 28-30
– and attainment 30, 37, 38, 39
Heath, S.B. 6, 7, 8
Heller, M. 1, 118, 128, 145, 146
Hewison, J. 27, 28, 30, 31, 32, 34
Hindko 98
Hindi 21
Hindu 15, 21
Hmong 5
home liaison teachers 135
home literacy observation 66
home visits 24, 30, 32, 35, 38, 51, 86, 135, 140
Hughes, M. 24
Hutchison, S. 50, 130

identity 1, 2, 12-14, 21, 57, 115-117, 122, 124, 128, 137, 138
ideology 13, 14
illiteracy 17, 18, 22, 56, 114
immigrant groups 4, 13, 14, 16, 46, 61
India 21
inequality 41, 59, 138
inspection of schools 23, 103
interpreters 51, 90, 91, 92, 97, 98, 100, 107, 145
interviews 67, 68

Jackson, A. 28, 33
Jackson, J. 33
Japanese 15
Japanese-American 14
Jones, B. 33
Jones, K. 5
Jowett, S. 24, 38, 51
Jungnitz, G. 35

Kamehameha Early Education Programme 8-10
Karran, S. 52, 94
Kashmiri 52
Kell, C. 19
Khmer 36, 37, 53
Kirklees Local Education Authority 35
Knight, A. 6, 128

Landau, J. 19
Lankshear, C. 19, 45, 46
Langer, J.A. 3, 11
Lao 53
Lareau, A. 44
Latino parents 58, 134, 135
Leach, D.J. 33, 37
Leicester 21, 139
letter-writing 4, 25, 116, 139
Lindsay, G. 34, 35
linguistic capital 43, 44, 94, 130, 131, 133, 136, 138, 146
Linguistic Minorities Project 15
literacy
– teachers' attitudes to 47-49, 110, 137
– parents' attitudes to 49-53, 77
– autonomous 16
– purposes 4, 110, 118, 119
– critical 17, 18, 124-126
– cultural 17
– functional 17, 18
– individual skills 2
– interpsychological 11
– intrapsychological 11
– motivation 8, 122
– process of 1-4, 39

– psychological 3
– social 1-3, 5, 19
– symbolic value 14, 15, 116, 117, 118, 120
local education authorities 24
Luke, A. 5, 6, 13
Lytle, S. 19

McConnell-Ginet, S. 128
McCormick, C.E. 26
MacDonald, I. 104
McNally, J. 26
McNaughton, S. 36, 48, 136
Macedo, D. 18, 21
madressa 50
Malay 62
Malawi 21
Martin-Jones, M. 4, 21, 68, 99, 139
Mason, J.M. 26
Massey, I. 104
Matute-Bianchi, M. E. 13, 14
methodological approaches 62-69
Mexican-American 4, 13
Mills, J. 98
Minns, H. 54
minority languages 54, 102, 103, 121, 122
Mirpuri 15, 98, 141
Moore, D. 118
Mortimore, J. 50
mosque 15, 66, 84, 118, 119
multiculturalism 18, 102-104
multilingualism 41, 102-104

National Child Development Study 26
Native-American 9, 10
Navajo 8, 9
New Zealand 36, 48, 49
Newman, D. 11
Newson, J. 26, 27
Newson, E. 26, 27

Ofsted 103
Ogbu, J. 16, 17
oral literacy 109, 110, 112
oral tradition 110
Osler, A. 101

Pakistan 15
Pakistani groups in Britain 15, 62, 98, 100, 104
paired reading 34, 35, 37, 38, 39
Panjabi 14, 53, 115
parental aspirations 78-80
parental involvement 23-28, 30, 32, 34-38, 40, 43-47, 105, 106, 107
parents' evenings 90-92
parents' workshops 93-95
Parr, J. 48
Passeron, J.C. 43
pause, prompt, praise 36-37
pedagogy 17-18, 103
Plewis, I. 27
policy-making 23, 41, 146
power
    – and literacy 16-17
    – minority and majority groups 6, 43
    – social and cultural reproduction of 1, 144
Powney, J. 68
professional development 99, 101
professionalisation of teaching 131-133
Pushto 15, 98

Quebec 118
Qur'an 15, 50, 84, 100, 118

racial abuse 52, 104-105
racism 104-105
read-at-home 49
reading
    – attainment 24-25, 25-28, 31-34, 123
    – at home 4-5, 30-34, 54-58, 75-78, 91, 113-114
    – at school 73-74
Reder, S. 2, 3, 5, 17, 77
Reese, L. 54
resistance 19, 21
resources for literacy learning 123-124
Robinson, V 48.

Sait, L 20
Sanskrit 21
SATs 103
Saxena, M. 5, 14, 115
Schofield, W.N. 30
school literacy observation 66
Scribner, S. 3, 5
siblings: as reading tutors 35, 53, 75-78, 83, 84
Siddall, S.W. 33, 37
Sikh 15
Simich-Dudgeon, C. 52, 53, 80
Sneddon, R. 52, 92
social justice 62, 103, 104, 105, 120-126, 142-146
social selection 145
sociocultural congruence 7-10
socioeconomic status
    – and reading attainment 7-8, 25-28, 47-49
South Africa 20, 21
Spanish 4, 5, 45, 46, 53, 55, 57, 67
Stierer, B. 24
Stokes, S. 4, 25, 111
storytelling 7, 10, 110-112
Street, B. 12, 16, 18, 19, 22, 114
Street, J. 19, 114
Sulzby, E. 3
Sylheti 13, 69, 90, 99, 110, 141

Taylor, D. 25
Taylor, I. 15
Teale, W.H. 3, 25
Tharp, R. 8, 10
teachers
    – attitudes to parents 47-49
    – expectations 96, 97, 112, 123, 127, 128, 133, 136, 140, 141
    – perceptions 46, 112, 137, 142
    – practices 28, 47, 82-83
Timperley, H. 48
Tizard, B. 24, 25, 27, 50
Tizard, J. 27, 28, 30, 31, 32
Tomlinson, S. 50, 130

Toomey, D. 34, 38, 49, 86, 138
Topping K. 34, 35, 38
Trinity-Arlington Project 53
Troyna, B. 104
Trueba, H. 11, 17, 77, 137
Turkish 51

Urdu 15, 98, 100, 103, 105, 110, 117, 118

Vietnamese 52
Vincent, C. 47, 50, 80, 92, 132, 136, 137
Vygotsky, L.S. 2, 4

Watts, M. 68
Weber R.-M. 61
Weinberger, J. 28
Wells, G. 25, 26
Williams, D.L 50, 80
Wolfendale, S. 24

Zentella, A.C. 17
zone of proximal development 2, 11, 12